My Country

Discovering North East England

Written and compiled by

Tony Henderson

The Journal

Our grateful thanks to the following photographers and organizations for the images used in this book: Barry Pells, Jayne Emsley, Tim McGuinness, Ian Winter, Paul Norris, Simon Hobson, Simon Greener, Mark Savage, The National Trust, English Heritage, Airfotos, Northumberland National Park, Northumberland Wildlife Trust and Laing Art Gallery.

All contact details, prices and site details are correct at time of publication.

First published in 2005 by: First Edition Limited, 32 Stamford Street, Altrincham, Cheshire, WA14 1EY in conjunction with The Journal, Thomson House, Groat Market, Newcastle NE1 1ED.

Images: © The Journal, unless otherwise stated.

©2005 The Journal.

ISBN: 1-84547-094-X

Contents

Foreword

At last someone has produced a comprehensive guide to North East England's extraordinary array of visitor attractions. Tony Henderson has scoured the region for the best coastline, gardens, castles, walks, monuments, museums, wildlife, hills, valleys, dales, forts, great halls, religious houses and just about everything else that could keep a visitor happy in this incredibly diverse region. He has covered the old favourites like Hadrian's Wall, Holy Island and Alnwick Castle but with a journalist's curiosity and endless stamina, he has delved into the secrets of the 'Land of Far Horizons', into the Cheviot Hills, where strange place names evoke powerful memories of bloody deeds perpetrated during 500 years of border warfare, to many lesser known places where the northern culture has left its unique character – and to new attractions, like the Alnwick Garden, which have added a new dimension for visitors

The secrets of Northumberland and its neighbouring counties have been well kept and visitors to the area are nearly always amazed at the unspoilt countryside and coastline and the wealth of heritage and history reflected in its architecture and archaeology. As visitors from all around the world discover the North East's charm and beauty, this book will be an essential guide.

Duke of Northumberland

Introduction

Of all the sayings bandied about there is one which has the ring of cast iron certainty.

"You never know what you've got till it's gone," and that surely applies to one of the North-East's greatest assets – its landscape, wild places and abundant heritage.

This is not to gloss over the fact that the region has its problems and that great efforts must be made to tackle and overcome them.

But it also has much of which it can be proud.

There are the Cheviot Hills and the North Pennine moors, where the nearest to wilderness in England can be found; designated Areas of Outstanding National Beauty along the Northumberland coast and the North Pennines; heritage coastline in Northumberland and County Durham; castles galore; one of the world's grandest cathedrals; historic towns and cities; two world heritage sites; the northernmost edge of the Roman Empire and in Hadrian's Wall one of its most impressive monuments; a national park; the Durham dales and a pivotal role in the history of European Christianity.

A study commissioned by the National Trust on the economic value of the environment in the North-East and Cumbria found that 40pc of the tourist economy depends on high quality, well maintained natural and cultural assets.

A total of 67,000 people in the North-East work in the tourism industry and 27,000 of these jobs rely directly on our natural and historic built environment.

What is on offer is a surprise to visitors or people locating to the region who have often been reared on outdated smokestack images.

Those from the North-East have long been clued in to the true picture. But even for locals, there is still much to explore and this book reveals just what is out there.

Tony Henderson, 2005.

Ford and Etal

A river which is home to otter and kingfisher powers the water mill which produces stoneground wholemeal flour.

In the thatched pub, opposite the thatched cottages and a short walk from the 14th Century castle, customers enjoy a leisurely drink. Sounds like a slice of old England, and southern England at that. It's England all right, but only just. Mill, pub, cottages and castle are part of the Ford and Etal estate, a few miles from the Scottish Border in the shadow of the Cheviot Hills in north Northumberland.

Ford and Etal, each with its own castle, are twin picturesque villages. In between is Heatherslaw Mill on the River Till – the only tributary of the River Tweed to be wholly within England.

Heatherslaw and Etal are linked by a 15-inch gauge steam railway whose tiny carriages are a child's – and many an adult's – delight. Heatherslaw is the most northerly working water mill in England and is run by a charitable trust.

Visitors can step inside and listen to the creaking and groaning of a grand old lady.

A document of 1306 records that Nicholas Graham's widow held a water mill at Heatherslaw worth £4 a year. The mill was rebuilt between 1768 and 1770 by Ford's then owner, Sir John Hussey Delaval. Fifty years later it was substantially altered and this is largely the mill which we see today.

Left: The Moses and Miriam mural at Lady Waterford Hall.

Below: Lady Waterford Hall, Ford. Built by Lady Waterford as a school for local children.

A central figure in the history of Ford was Louisa Anne, Marchioness of Waterford. She was born in 1818 in Paris, where her father was British ambassador.

At a tournament in Ayrshire in 1842, she met Henry, 3rd Marquess of Waterford, who owned Ford and large estates in Ireland and they were married in the same year. But in 1859 he was killed in a hunting accident in Ireland. Lady Waterford set up home at Ford Castle and rebuilt Ford as a model village. Although as a supporter of temperance she closed the village's Delaval Arms pub, she built a school for the local children, which has become one of the region's most unusual attractions. Lady Waterford was a keen artist who produced more than 600 works and between 1862 and 1883 she personally decorated the school walls with huge murals on Biblical themes. She used people from the village and the estate as models for the murals. In effect, the school walls became a portrait gallery of local people over a period of 21 years. The model for the figure of the Child Saviour was Jimmy Locke, the son of a miner at Ford Moss Colliery. He became a miner himself, working at Scremerston near Berwick. He died in 1939, aged 64. David the Shepherd was Peter Rule, whose father was a slater at Ford. Peter himself was to set up in business as a butcher in the years to come.

Also in the murals is Mrs Mary Heslop, who worked at Ford Castle for 69 years, 23 as housekeeper to Lady Waterford, a post she held until her death at the age of 92 in 1882. The figure of Josiah is said to have been modelled by Willie Oliver, who later ran what is now the Friendly Hound pub at Ford Common.

Next to Lady Waterford Hall is a two-acre nursery in what was the walled garden of Ford Castle.

Visitors can stroll around the gardens and buy plants, many of which can be seen growing in the borders.

The site of the Battle of Flodden lies within the Ford and Etal estate. Both Ford and Etal castles were taken in 1513 by an invading army of 30,000 men led by the Scottish King James IV. The army included the flower of Scottish aristocracy, with 15 earls and 20 barons.

The 70-year-old Earl of Surrey gathered an opposing army of 26,000 at Newcastle and was allowed by the Prior of Durham to carry the banner of St Cuthbert. The Earl led the army across the River Till and surprised the Scots by taking up a position to their north, cutting off their line of retreat back across the border. At 4.15pm on September 9, the battle began and after only two hours 9,000 Scots lay dead, including almost the entire ruling class.

English losses were put at between 1,500 and 3,000. The battle was fought around Branxton Hill, a couple of miles or so from Etal. On a rise in front of the village of Branxton stands a memorial cross, erected early last century to the brave of both nations.

Branxton Parish Council has improved access and information for visitors in a project backed by a £24,970 Local Heritage Initiative grant and £5,000 from the Nationwide Building Society. A battlefield trail has been created and seating provided.

In 1949, the millstones stopped turning and the building fell into dereliction. But the trust was set up in 1972 and three years later the mill opened to the public.

The mill grinds wheat from the estate and produces 20 tonnes of wholemeal flour a year, which is sold to visitors, around 50 small businesses and Fenwick's store in Newcastle. Flour also goes to the Heatherslaw Bakery directly opposite, whose cakes and biscuits are on sale. The mill also sells barley and oat products. As home breadmaking increases, demand has risen for the flour, with the result that the mill is producing twice what it did six years ago.

It could turn out a lot more - three tonnes a day in fact.

Julia Nolan, who lives in Milfield near Wooler, has worked at the mill for 10 years - the last five as head miller.

She says: "The mill has her own character and her own moods. When you are so old you can be forgiven a bit of eccentricity and stubbornness.

"At times she wants to go faster but she is an old lady and we are trying to protect and preserve her."

The mill, with the Granary cafe next door, attracts around 10,000 visitors a year and youngsters can become junior millers, with certificates to prove it, by answering questions based on a tour of the building.

Leaving the mill, the best way to reach Etal is to chug along the railway. There you will find the Black Bull, the only thatched pub in Northumberland. The

Ford village.

Above: Heatherslaw Corn Mill still uses traditional methods and machinery to grind locally grown wheat.

Left: Julia Nolan, head miller at Heatherslaw Mill.

ruins of the castle are testimony to the years of Border warfare and local feuding.

The 15,000-acre estate, run by Lord Joicey, is also home to ventures such as nursery gardens, a pottery, smithy and furniture maker, plus 32 farms and 1,480 acres of woodland. Lord Joicey is the latest in a long line of landowners at Ford and Etal.

In the 14th Century, the manor of Ford was held by the Heron family and Etal by the Manners clan.

Ford Castle is now a field study and residential centre operated by Northumberland County Council and Etal Castle is in the care of English Heritage.

In times of Border conflict, both were built to defend key crossings south over the River Till. But the Scots were not the only worry. The neighbours could be just as troublesome. In 1428 William Heron attacked Etal Castle and was killed in the clash. John Manners had to pay Heron's widow a sum of money and fund the saying of 500 masses for Heron's soul.

In the 19th and early 20th Century, new wealth was concentrated in the hands

Left: Heatherslaw Light Railway is a 15 gauge steam and diesel light railway on the Ford and Etal estate.

Right: This horseshoe door is one of the more unusual architectural features in Ford village.

of the industrialists and Etal was sold in 1885 to Sunderland shipowner James Laing.

In 1907, Ford was bought by the first Lord Joicey, a mineowner and MP for Chester-le-Street. Lord Joicey bought Etal and united them under one ownership for the first

time. His great grandson, the present Lord Joicey, says that visitors help support a viable rural community.

He says: "There are all sorts of gems to be found at Ford and Etal, but then north Northumberland and the North-East have many undiscovered gems."

Ford and Etal are reached from the A1. Take the B6353 through Fenwick and Lowick, following the signs for Ford and Etal.

Alternatively, use the A697, taking the B6354 from Wooler.

Lady Waterford Hall is open daily from April to November 10.30am-12pm and 1.30pm-5.30pm.

Admission adult £1.75, concessions £1.25, child over 12, 75p.

Telephone 01890 820 503.

Ford plant nursery is open Monday to Friday 9am-4.30pm and weekends from March to October 10am-6pm. Telephone 01890 820 379.

Heatherslaw Mill is open daily March 12 to September 10am-6pm, October 10am-5pm. Adult £3, concessions £1.50, family ticket £7.50.

Telephone 01890 820 338.

The site also has a café, visitor centre, shop and bakery.

Heatherslaw Light Railway runs daily from 11.30am-3.30pm from Easter to the end of October. Adults £5 return, child over three £3, concessions £4.

Telephone 01890 820 317.

Etal Castle is open daily April to September 30, 10am-6pm, October-March closed Adult £3, concessions £2.30, child £1.50, family ticket £7.50.

Telephone 01890 820 332.

Tony Henderson

Left: A stunning view of the Cheviot Hills taken from College Valley.

College Valley

Once I had a conversation with a historian who had written a book on life in England a thousand years ago.

It revolved around what the reaction of people from that time would be if they could be brought back to experience the world we live in now.

"Of all the modern trappings of our everyday existence – TVs, aircraft, cars, cameras, mobile phones, computers and so on – what single item would be the biggest shock to our time travellers?", I asked.

"Noise", was the reply.

Mark Savage

The tranquil College Valley nestled in the Cheviot Hills offers a solitude rarely found in our modern, hectic lives.

Mark Savage

At one time there 18 shepherds and nine farms in College Valley. And 40 years ago forestry was high profile with the planting of conifer blocks on 1,600 acres. Now there are just two farm tenancies and one shepherd.

The conifers, now considered unsightly, are being thinned out. The aim of College Valley Estates Ltd is to convert about half of the conifer land to native broadleaf woodland. At Harrowbog there's already the largest area of ancient semi-natural woodland in Northumberland National Park.

But Colin Matheson, agent and secretary to College Valley Estates, is mindful of the resident red squirrel population. Felling all the conifers would be detrimental to the squirrels so a bid to strike a balance includes "wilderness" woodland planting on 200 acres of the slope of Cheviot.

While farming and forestry are ongoing the focus is on conservation, recreation and education. The 12,000-acre estate was bought in 1953 by CVE, whose parent company is Samares Investments.

This was the original commercial company of Tyneside philanthropist Sir James Knott. He left a large legacy for good works through the James Knott Trust. Born at Howdon, now North Tyneside, in 1855, he would no doubt have approved of CVE's aim to enhance the valley.

The move towards broadleaf woodland has encouraged return of the rare black grouse, and trails have been created linking the hillforts.

Compared to life way back, most of us today live against a background of incredibly constant noise, even if we have grown used to much of it. The place which our noise-numbed ancestors would

most feel at home today would be the College Valley in the Cheviot Hills in Northumberland.

We may live in car-crazy times, but only 12 vehicles a day are allowed into the valley, and then only by permit. The permit system means that, in effect, the valley is traffic-free. Truly a place to prize.

The resultant solitude is the backdrop to what is perhaps the nearest to a touch of wilderness there is to be found in England. It is a valley, flanked by hills topped by eight hillforts from 2,300 years ago, where the prehistoric landscape is everywhere. The valley leads to the great mass of Cheviot itself. The resident population is only around 30 and there is the merest scattering of buildings.

The only folk you are likely to meet are drivers at the car park at the valley entrance at Hethpool, and the occasional walker. That all adds up to getting away from it all in a fashion that is an increasingly rare experience in today's crowded society.

Exploring the College Valley has been likened to coming up against a great piece of music, book or work of art.

There is the first huge impact and then the pleasure of returning to it

and finding something a little different each time.

The view from within the tumbled ramparts of Great Hetha hillfort in the College Valley is a powerful panorama which takes in the bulk of Cheviot and also encompasses the surrounding hills of Easter Tor and Wester Tor, Hare Law, Coldburn Hill, North Blackhaggs, Eli's Knowe, Preston Hill and Loft Hill.

Then there are the nearby hillforts of Little Hetha, Sinkside Hill, Ring Chesters, West Hill, Mid

Mark Savage

Far left: College Burn.

Left: Hethpool Stone Circle in College Valley.

The debate goes on over the function of these hillforts. Were they purely defensive or were they built to impress the neighbours?

At Staw Hill, the section of wall facing the nearby hillfort of Mid Hill was large and elaborate but the opposite stretch was lower and more simply constructed.

Cultivation terraces, some of which may date back 4,000 years, line the hills as if the slopes have been raked by a giant comb.

Archaeologists have found that some of the hillforts, like Ring Chesters, were built on top of earlier settlements which had been protected by timber palisades.

At West Hill, which commands the eastern approach to the valley, evidence suggests that the hillfort was occupied by an extended family of 15 to 20 people.

At the hamlet of Hethpool on the valley floor, there are the remains of a prehistoric stone circle. Hethpool suffered in the Anglo-Scottish wars. In 1343 it was "devastated" and was attacked again before the Battle of Flodden in 1513.

Deeper into the College Valley is a memorial to the Allied airmen who lost their lives in plane crashes in the Cheviot Hills during the Second World War.

Princess Anne unveiled the valley's Animals in War memorial. Among those it honours is Sheila owned by shepherd John Dagg, who helped save crew of an American Flying Fortress bomber which came down on the summit of Cheviot. Bad weather had forced it to abandon a bombing mission to Germany, but it became lost and crashed on Cheviot. The fuel and ammunition caught fire.

Two crew members died but four escaped, stumbling into a gully. Mr Dagg and another shepherd, Frank Moscrop, heard the crash and set off up the hill with Sheila running ahead. Three hours later one of the crew looked up and felt Sheila licking his face. Her barking led the shepherds to the men and they made bandages from parachute silk then helped them down the hill. Mr Dagg's daughter cycled down the valley to raise the alarm.

The shepherds received the British Empire Medal and Sheila was awarded the animals' VC, the Dicken Medal. The mother of Frank Turner, one of the airmen who died, wrote to the shepherds to thank them and added that if Sheila ever had pups she would like one. A pup was eventually flown out by the RAF to Mrs Turner in South Carolina and became town pet.

Two of the survivors were present in 1993 when the valley's airmen memorial was unveiled by the Duke of Gloucester.

Also there was Jim Beasom, rear gunner and sole survivor of a Halifax bomber which crashed in the Cheviots in 1945.

Other pilots who lost their lives in crashes in the area are buried in cemetery of Kirknewton village near the mouth of the valley.

Hill, Staw Hill and Yeavering Bell.

There is also the sense of place and history. These are the same ramparts, whose stones still lie where they fell, behind which Iron Age people lived. Traces of the sites of their timber roundhouses can still be seen.

In 1596 it was hit by a band of Reivers including Kerrs, Youngs and Burns clan members.

One of the later landowners was Admiral Lord Collingwood, who, for his part in the Battle of Trafalgar, was made Baron of Caldburne and Hethpole.

One of the finest walks in Northumberland leads to a legacy of the great man. It starts from the village of Kirknewton, with its impressive St Gregory's Church, passing the former railway station built when a branch line was opened from Alnwick to Coldstream in 1887. It closed to passenger traffic in 1930 when it succumbed to competition from the motor bus.

The walk descends from Westnewton bridge to follow the lovely College

Burn, with its brown trout, to Hethpool Linn waterfall. Facing the waterfall is the hill of Hethpool Bell. Collingwood was a great lover of trees and, while he was at sea, his wife Sarah began the planting project he had decided upon.

Oaks were planted on Hethpool Bell to provide timber for the nation's warships. But Collingwood would have been disappointed, for thin soil and exposed conditions have resulted in stunted and bent specimens.

Near the valley entrance is Hethpool House with its conical tower and lake,

built in the Arts and Crafts style for Tyneside shipping company owner Sir Arthur Munro Sutherland on the site of a 17th Century home.

Sir Arthur, who bought Hethpool in 1918, was Lord Mayor of Newcastle and Sheriff of Northumberland.

He also owned the Newcastle Chronicle and was president of the Chamber of Shipping.

His was a distinguished and busy career.

But it was in the College Valley that he found peace and contentment.

Hethpool is reached from the A697 near Wooler.

Take the B6351 off the A697.

Just after Kirknewton, take the minor road to Hethpool.

Northumberland National Park has published a booklet of four walking trails in the College Valley. Tel: (01434) 605555.

Aerial view of the dramatic Iron Age hillfort, Yeavering Bell.

Yeavering Bell

The barrier of thousands of years means we will never know for sure how the landscape "spoke" to our ancestors.

But all the evidence suggests that they singled out certain places as being very special indeed – even sacred.

And perhaps the most sacred of them all is a hill on the edge of the Cheviot Hills in Northumberland National Park.

The twin peaks of Yeavering Bell loom over the Milfield Plain near Wooler and the rivers Glen and Till.

In the other direction, behind Yeavering Bell, is the entirely different and dramatic landscape of the Cheviot Hills.

Research has shown that between 4,000 and 5,000 years ago a circular henge monument - an open-air ceremonial site - was created at Milfield North so that the view from its southern entrance was directly aligned on Yeavering Bell.

Two thousand years later, 12 acres of the summit of

The Ad Gefrin palace layout beneath Yeavering Bell is arguably one of the most important Anglo-Saxon sites in the country. The site had already been in use for thousands of years with a henge monument, cremation cemetery and burial mound, that was still visible when the palace complex was constructed and which the builders respected and incorporated.

Although the site was referred to by Bede, it was an aerial photograph taken in the very dry summer of 1949 which alerted archaeologists to the tantalising prospect that here was something outstanding.

The distinguished archaeologist Brian Hope-Taylor began excavations in the early 1950s and started to piece together the components of the palace site.

A Great Hall was built about 627. Brian Hope-Taylor, drawing on the legend of Beowulf, speculated that the hall was used for feasting, drinking and ceremonies.

He also excavated what looked like a triangular, tiered grandstand, or theatre.

Those seated in the theatre faced a stage, which itself was backed by a screen to the rear and either side.

It was likely to have been the venue where the king addressed his followers or the court held their meetings.

What is described as the Great Enclosure may have been built in prehistoric or Roman times and was already ancient when the palace buildings went up. It may have been used as a corral for cattle and horses paid as taxes by people living in the surrounding area, or a place for communal ceremonies.

The Anglo-Saxon base probably played a similar role as that of the hillfort – as a power centre from which the adjoining lands were ruled.

The site became one of great Christian significance, as Bede writes about how Paulinus spent 36 days preaching and baptising people in the River Glen.

Edwin, who was King of Northumbria from 616 until 633, married the Kentish princess Ethelburga.

A condition was that she could bring her chaplain, Paulinus, who had been sent to England from Rome by Pope Gregory the Great. Paulinus went on to spread the Christian message in Northumbria and Edwin was baptised.

But he was killed in battle against King Penda of Mercia, who with the help of the Welsh king Cadwallon defeated the Northumbrians, and there is clear evidence that the palace site was put to the torch.

Excavations showed that scorch marks at the base of the theatre were consistent with brushwood being piled up against the timberwork.

Hope-Taylor said: "The disaster is surely to be seen as a result of a calculated act of hostility. Overall the evidence speaks of a desperate last stand by defenders loyal to all the township had stood for."

Yeavering Bell was covered with at least 130 timber roundhouses making it the biggest and the most imposing hillfort in the North of England.

And it was no mere coincidence that for 100 years from the late sixth century, land at the base of Yeavering Bell was used as the site of an Anglian royal palace which played a pivotal role in the conversion of Northumbria to Christianity.

"For around 3,000 years this area is a major regional focal point. Yeavering Bell is a special place from the Stone Age to the seventh century," says national park archaeologist Paul Frodsham.

That sort of presence does not go away. Today, those who make the effort to climb the meandering trail up 1,000ft Yeavering Bell can sample it for themselves.

"There is a specialness about Yeavering Bell which is indefinable and people who go up can experience it in their own way," says Paul.

The Anglo-Saxon palace site has been bought by local archaeologist Roger Miket to preserve it for future generations and to allow access for visitors today.

Roger was engaged in a number of digs in the North-East, including one at an Anglo-Saxon settlement at Thirlings, near Yeavering. The palace site is managed by the Gefrin Trust.

Roger bought the land from a local farming family when it came on to the market.

"It has a wonderful story to tell but it has not been telling it very well," says Roger.

Trustee Chris Burgess, archaeologist with Northumberland County Council, says: "It was the seat of royal power for the best part of 100 years and is one of the sites of the birth of Christianity in the North of England yet few people know it exists or have any concept of how important it is."

Chris believes that the palace arena drew on the power of Yeavering Bell and was itself built on a "hogback" of land which overlooked the river and the plain, from which the king could look down on where his subjects lived and worked.

Yeavering Bell, part of the dramatic Cheviot landscape

Bede, who wrote about the Anglo-Saxon palace site, called it Ad Gefrin.

Gefrin, an old British word, is pronounced Yevrin and means the Hill of the Goats.

On the way up the hill, walkers can see the feral goats, with the billys sporting goatee beards and fine horns.

"The Hill of the Goats must have been the name which the Iron Age people who lived on Yeavering Bell used for the hillfort," says Paul.

"But you wouldn't name the most important hillfort in the North of England just because there were goats there.

The "city in the sky" hillfort was occupied between 2,300 and 3,000 years ago. It would have been spectacular.

The andersite rock, quarried from the hill to build the fort's ramparts was bright pink when fresh.

Even now, after centuries of weathering have turned it grey, traces of the original pink can be glimpsed.

"The wild goats must have been a totemic animal with ritual significance for the people at the time."

Often, when the Anglo-Saxons took over important British sites, they re-named them. But at Yeavering, when they built their palace settlement, they kept the local and probably powerful name of Gefrin.

From the top of Yeavering Bell today there are the sweeping views - to the North Sea in fine weather - and back the other way into the Cheviots which the hillfort dwellers would have experienced.

The imprints of their roundhouses can still be detected. But where once there was the bustle of everyday life from 130 homes, all is now silent save for the breeze and the curlew calls.

The people are long gone, yet something of them remains.

"Today people go up Yeavering Bell as a break from their busy lives. But it was home to the Iron Age people," says Paul.

He believes that with the coming of Christianity, features such as Yeavering Bell lost some of their ritual meaning.

When worship could take place in a church built anywhere, there was less need for a specific, sacred site in the landscape.

But in recent years there has been a re-awakening of appreciation of the spiritual qualities of such places.

That local folk memory persisted is suggested by the name given to a bastle house - a defensible dwelling - built around 1600 at the foot of Yeavering Bell and which was called the Old Palace.

Paul says: "It was always a very important site. There is something very distinctive about the appearance of Yeavering Bell.

"It is in a stunning landscape setting and there is this hazy understanding of what happened there many generations ago.

"That is why people go there today and it was the same hazy memory for the people of the past."

Answers to questions such as when the hillfort was abandoned may be answered in a hoped-for research project on the site which is being talked about in the longer-term.

George Tate, the first archaeologist known to have excavated at Yeavering Bell in 1862, wrote: "We are groping our way through a dark period ... the people who lived then had little to leave behind them."

But on the top of Yeavering Bell, sheltering behind the tumbled, once-pink ramparts, what are remote times can seem surprisingly close.

Yeavering Bell is reached via the B6351 off the A697 near Wooler.

The hillfort is a protected monument and is managed under an agreement between Northumberland National Park and the landowner.

The park authority has produced a leaflet guide to the three and a half mile walk to the summit. Tel: (01434) 605555.

The Ad Gefrin site is off the B6351 a short distance before the start of the walk.

Further details on the site are available on a website set up by Northumberland and Durham county councils with backing from the New Opportunities Fund to highlight the history and archaeology of the areas.

Go to www.pastperfect.info

Dramatic view across the Milfield Plain towards the Cheviots.

Milfield Plain

Fanning out from the edge of the Cheviot Hills in Northumberland is the Milfield Plain, a fertile area crossed by the rivers Till and Glen.

It is the third component of a spiritual landscape which includes the hillforts of the Cheviots, the sacred 1,000ft Yeavering Bell with its twin summits and an Anglo-Saxon palace site at its base.

The Milfield Plain near Wooler is special in its own right, not least because it is one of the best prehistoric landscapes in the country. Evidence for some of the earliest agriculture in Northern England from around 6,000 years ago has been found there. It also happens to have one of the most dense concentrations of henge monuments in Britain. So far nine henges have been discovered on the Milfield Plain, with most dating from around 4,500 years ago.

Henges are ritual, circular monuments formed by an outer mound or bank and an inner ditch with one or two entrances. Sometimes they contained an inner feature of burials and stone or wooden uprights. The plain attracted people from the Stone Age onwards.

As the Ice Age sheets melted, large volumes of gravel were washed down from the Cheviot Hills and spread out like a river delta. The glacial meltwaters formed a large lake extending over what is now the floodplain of the Till and the Glen. As the lake eventually drained away, people moved in to exploit the abundant natural resources. They began to rear livestock and grow food plants to supplement hunting and fishing.

Overlooking the Milfield Plain, Wooler, and the rock art sandstone ridges is a hill which has been at the centre of history. The 900ft Humbleton Hill, also called Homildon in medieval times, was the site of one of the hillforts which form a ring around the edge of the Cheviots. It was one of the most strongly defended hillforts in the area, with its pink stone ramparts being built around 300BC. The barrier has mostly collapsed into a spread of stones but, when new, it would have been 6ft high and 10ft wide, circling at least 20 huts.

The fact that Bronze age burials were found at the base of the hill suggest that it was already an important place 4,000 years ago. Another name for the hill was Hameldun, which is old English for Cleft Hill. This stems from the steep-sided ravine on the south side of the hill, which is now a geological site of special scientific interest. It is suspected that the hill was reoccupied in the Fifth Century when local war bands ruled the roost.

Humbleton Hill went on to feature in Shakespeare's Henry IV Part I after a battle fought on and around its slopes in 1402. A Scots force of around 10,000, led by Archibald, Earl of Douglas, had attacked Northern England while Henry IV was fighting Owen Glendower in Wales. As the Scots headed homewards with their booty, they found their way barred by the Earl of Northumberland, Henry Percy, and his son Hotspur.

The Percys took up a position five miles north west of Wooler and Douglas deployed his men on the sides of Humbleton Hill. The Earl of Northumberland then drew up his force on the plain at the foot of the hill and despatched his longbowmen up nearby Harehope Hill.

The longbow, whose prowess had been proved in several earlier battles, again proved the telling factor. Arrows rained down on Humbleton, transfixing "the hands and arms of the Scots to their own lances," according to sources. This forced many of the Scots down the hill to attack the English, but the archers kept up their barrage.

Douglas suffered five wounds, and the Scots were routed, with hundreds drowning as they tried to swim the River Tweed. The killing fields are still known as Red Riggs, from the blood of the fallen Scots and human skulls, other bones and the skeletons of horses have been ploughed up over the years.

Newcastle University archaeologist Clive Waddington has carried out extensive research and excavation on Milfield Plain.

He says: "The area is clearly a focus for the earliest inhabitants because of the fertile soil and also because they had access to a wide range of resources."

These included different types of stone, such as the hard volcanic Cheviot rock for axes, and flint from the gravels for tools. There were salmon in the rivers, deer and wild cattle in the varying woodlands and birds such as swans, ducks and geese.

"The plain is also in the rain shadow of the Cheviots and so has a lower annual rainfall and longer hours of sunshine," says Clive.

The climate generally was better than today. Dr Malcolm Aylett, now retired but who was a GP in Wooler for 25 years, is former chairman of the Border Archaeological Society.

He says: "The plain would have been rich in food and the living would have been quite easy."

Left: The interior of a reconstructed Prehistoric Hut.
Above: A reconstruction of the Milfield North henge.

"It would have been a comfortable life for the times.

"It is, arguably, one of the most important and richest sites archaeologically in England.

"From the top of the hills, its origin as a vast lake is so obvious."

Society vice chairman Barrie Evans tells how members hired an aircraft to fly over the area.

"The henges stood out like huge signposts," he says.

By building the henges, says Clive, people laid a spiritual and ritual layer on the landscape.

The henges are in a line across the plain, and probably served as a processional way or sacred route.

The first, Milfield North, is aligned on Yeavering Bell and nearby Humbleton Hill, which are the most prominent hills on the edge of the Cheviots.

Clive estimates that it would have taken a full day to process through the henges to Yeavering Bell – the site of the last henge – and back again.

In outlying areas such as Duddo, Doddington Moor and Threestone Burn, there are stone circles.

The Duddo circle has a number of standing stones which have been sculpted by centuries of wind and rain. There is speculation that the circles and henges were used at different times of the year.

"If you lived in what is now Berwick, for example, everyone would have known about and gone to Milfield at least once in their lives, or perhaps every year.

"It was the big centre of gravity," says Clive.

"What is so special is that so much of this landscape is still intact. It is one of the best possible laboratories in which to try and understand what all this was about."

Bronze Age finds, including swords and axes, have come from the plain area and after the Anglo-Saxon palace site at the foot of Yeavering Bell was destroyed by fire when the

Bracketing the Milfield Plain are sandstone ridges and moorland which harbour their own prehistoric surprises. They are studded with panels of rock art, created 4,000 to 5,000 years ago. The most spectacular example is at Roughting Linn, near Kimmerston.

Roughting Linn is named after a small nearby waterfall, and is a large domed sandstone outcrop 6oft long and 4oft wide. The symbol-covered rock, looking towards the Milfield Plain, is the biggest decorated slab in Northern England. It was once even bigger, but half as much again was quarried away. According to rock art expert Stan Beckensall, this is one of the most important sites of its type in the world.

The rock is in a partly-hollow ancient routeway leading to the Milfield Plain and the coast in the opposite direction.

The waterfall, trackway and the whaleback of rock made it a key location in the landscape.

More carvings at Broomridge lead to Goatscrag Hill, where there are further rock art and animal figures etched on to the wall of the hill's rock shelter, under the floor of which burials were discovered. Dod Law on Doddington Moor, Buttony, West Horton, the Ringses hillfort and Weetwood and Fowberry moors all have their panels, making the area the home of one of the most dense clusters of rock art in Britain. The proliferation of rock art, together with the henges, reinforces the feeling that this was a prime area for prehistoric people.

Stan says: "It would have been rich in food. The priority in any area is to get a living from it. It was a good place to live. It suited prehistoric people very well.

"When you mark the rocks you are saying 'this belongs to us' and perhaps you are marking places which are important to you."

People moving around the landscape would almost certainly have followed natural features like cliffs, ridges and rivers. The rock art appears in places which were prominent and would have been passed frequently by people on the move.

Another clue comes from what can be seen from the rock art sites. "There are fantastic views in all directions. You can see the Cheviots, the Milfield Plain and other sandstone scarps," says Stan.

"What is important is what you can see when you get there and that must have determined the choice of sites in the first place."

Northumbrians were defeated in battle, a new and similar power centre was built at Maelmin near the modern village of Milfield.

Reconstructions of the Milfield North henge and a hut shelter from up to 10,000 years ago which was excavated at the coast at Howick have been created at the Maelmin heritage trail site. Part of the work on the henge was carried out by Clive and a team of volunteers using the tools of the time, such as stone axes, digging sticks and the shoulder blades of cattle as primitive shovels.

Another insight into prehistoric life in the area was provided by an investigation undertaken by Border Archaeological Society members at a pear-shaped cairn on the side of Scald Hill at nearby Langleeford.

Barrie says: "There is a lot of pink andesite rock and quartz in there and it would have gleamed on the flanks of the hill. "It would have said: 'This land is ours'."

Northumberland National Park has produced a leaflet guide to a four-mile Humbleton Hill trail.

Telephone (01434) 605555.

The Maelmin heritage site is reached off the A697 by taking the signposted turning for Milfield village.

The trail car park is on the immediate right.

The Palladian Chapel on the Gibside Estate

Gibside Estate

There was a bride of 14 and a countess kidnapped at gunpoint by her husband after she sued for divorce.

Later, the family history included an earl who fell for a lord's daughter said to have danced naked at a regimental ball, and who then set up home with a housemaid.

The story of the Gibside estate near Rowlands Gill on the edge of Gateshead is peppered with love matches and fraught relationships which would not be out of place in a paperback novel. The tangled lives are as much a backdrop to the National Trust estate as the landscape and the historic buildings they left behind.

Remarkably, the 500-acre estate which reflects the 18th and 19th centuries is only three miles from the Gateshead MetroCentre.

The romantic shell of the estate's Gibside House bears the coat of arms of William Blakiston and his wife Jane's initials, and was the couple's home in the 1620s. Gibside passed to the Bowes family with the marriage of the couple's granddaughter Elizabeth to Sir William Bowes of Streatlam Castle in County Durham.

Sir William had a passion for horse racing – a trait which stayed in the family – and the 1675 Bowes Cup, the earliest known gold racing cup in Britain, is now in the Victoria and Albert Museum in London. Elizabeth had 10 children

Above: The Chapel interior featuring the unusual three-tier pulpit.

Above: Gibside by JMW Turner.

Right: An exteriot view of Gibside Hall.

the Long Walk, was given to the trust in 1974 and 19 years later the organisation acquired 353 acres of the park with the help of a National Heritage Memorial Fund grant. The purchase included Gibside House, the Column of Liberty, and the Orangery.

In 1997 the trust added nearby Cut Thorn Farm, a working stud, and one aim is to house some of its horses in the estate stables. The stables have also been converted into accommodation for volunteers and an exhibition and educational area telling the story of the estate.

The Column of Liberty has been restored and four walks – there were once 19 across the estate – have been created.

What are now rare daffodils, planted by Mary Eleanor, have bloomed again as undergrowth was cleared and there are longer term plans to restore and plant out the Orangery and the walled garden.

Property manager Tony Walton says: "What is absolutely amazing is that Gibside is just a 10-minute drive from the Gateshead MetroCentre and the aim is to make many more people aware of what is here, and that they can walk in lovely surroundings and in complete safety with their families."

Gibside's 18th Century chapel, which has stunning views down a tree-lined walkway, is frequently used for weddings and was also the setting for one of Magnus Magnusson's TV Mastermind shows.

Over recent years the trust has increased its holding at Gibside from 180 to 500 acres and visitor numbers have risen from 26,000 a year to 94,000.

By the 1950s Gibside was in steep decline. Gibside House, which had been used by land girls in the First World War, was abandoned and lost its roof and floors. The chapel may have followed suit but was restored by the trust in 1965. The building, together with

after the marriage and before she came into her inheritance, she died.

George set to work with a will to fashion his grand estate, and much of what visitors enjoy today is down to him.

In what were the outer pleasure grounds he built the Banqueting House, overlooking the Octagonal Pond which, with the Lily Pond, provides the estate's water features.

The Banqueting House had a Great Room for eating and drinking, and with George being a music lover and harpsichord player it was also ideal for concerts.

By 1751 George had completed his impressive stable block with its Palladian frontage and the Long Walk - now lined by Turkey Oaks and one of Gibside's most striking attractions.

in 12 years and the 18th Century Gibside estate was shaped by one of her sons, George, over a period of 40 years. George added to his wealth through exploiting

coal on his lands and there was the prospect of further enrichment when he married heiress Eleanor Verney, aged 14. But in 1725, just three months

The Hollow Walk continues the Long Walk and together they add up to a mile with Gibside Chapel and what qualifies as the first Statue of Liberty at either end.

George wanted the 120ft high Column of Liberty to advertise his support for the Whig Party and from its summit a 12ft statue of a young woman, with the Staff of Maintenance and the Cap of Liberty - symbols associated with Britannia - looks out over the estate. The statue was gilded with 66 books of gold leaf. George also tucked away a bath house on the estate and built a walled garden.

Eighteen years after the death of his first wife, George married another heiress, Mary Gilbert, and was almost 50 when their daughter Mary Eleanor was born. A year before his death George began work on Gibside Chapel as a place of worship and a family mausoleum.

As an heiress herself, Mary Eleanor was not short of suitors and on her 18th birthday in 1767 she married John Lyon, 9th Earl of Strathmore, who agreed to change his name to Bowes Lyon. The family produced the Queen Mother, daughter of the 14th Earl, and who visited Gibside for picnics as a young woman. Mary Eleanor's mother did not approve of the match, with the 9th Earl, complaining of "disorder in the family, many brothers and sisters, and lastly his being a Scotchman". Although

Mary Eleanor and John had five children, the union was not entirely happy and she began an affair with George Grey, by whom she became pregnant.

After the Earl's death in his late 30s from TB the countess, a passionate botanist, built what is now known as the Orangery, with seven bays of Tuscan columns to contain her exotic plants. She may have been well advised to concentrate on her horticultural pursuits, for her next love excursion was to prove disastrous. She married Andrew Robinson Stoney, an Irish adventurer said to be the model for the roguish hero of William Thackeray's novel Barry Lyndon, which in 1975 was turned into the film of the same name by Stanley Kubrick.

Mary Eleanor's pregnancy and relationship with Grey had been featured in the Morning Post, and she had been impressed by Stoney's offer to fight a duel with the editor.

But Stoney was infuriated to later find that Mary Eleanor had legally ensured that she kept hold of the estate and its income and as the relationship became increasingly unbearable, she fled to London and sued for divorce.

She was seized from her coach in Oxford Street and

Right: A family enjoy a day out at Gibside. In the background the Column of Liberty.

after a 33-hour journey north Stoney demanded at pistol point that she drop the divorce suit. With the alarm now raised, Stoney took his wife, still at pistol point, to Newcastle where he was arrested and later imprisoned.

Mary Eleanor's son John became the 10th Earl and in 1790 he attended a theatrical performance at Seaton Delaval Hall in south Northumberland, where he was enraptured by Lord Delaval's daughter Sarah.

It was she who was said to have enlivened the proceedings at the regimental ball, and who, although married to the Earl of Tyrconnel, was also the lover of Frederick, Duke of York, and a frequent visitor to Gibside to see the 10th Earl. She died at Gibside from TB at the age of 37.

Nine years later the Earl met Mary Milner, a Teesdale housemaid. She became his mistress and gave birth to a son, John, in 1811. The day before his death in 1820, the Earl was carried into church in a sedan chair and married Mary.

He is buried in the crypt at Gibside Chapel alongside George Bowes and Mary Eleanor.

Gibside is three miles west of the MetroCentre off the B6315 and six miles south west of Gateshead.

It is signposted from the Western Bypass.

The grounds are open all year, 10am-6pm from March 7 – October 23 and October 24-March 5 until 4pm, otherwise. Gibside is closed on Mondays although open on Bank Holiday Mondays.

Admission is £3.50 adult, £2 child, £10 family ticket. There is a tea room and shop. Telephone estate office (01207) 541820; tea room (01207) 541828; shop (01207) 541829.

Left: The bank at Barnard Castle

Head south to Barnard Castle in County Durham, gateway to Teesdale, and at its heart is, as the name suggests, an imposing 12th Century castle. But turn a corner at the 18th Century market cross and there, in a market town, is a full blown French chateau.

It is another of the family's surprises – this time the work of John Bowes, whose own life was far from orthodox.

As a nine-year-old boy, John had accompanied the body of his father, the 10th Earl of Strathmore, to his Gibside estate for burial in the chapel. With him was his mother Mary, who was a housemaid when the earl met her and who became his wife on the day before his death in 1820.

The young John became the owner of Gibside and Streatlam Castle in County Durham. He shared the family love of racehorses and his stud produced four Derby winners, including West Australian, the first winner of the Triple Crown in 1853. As well as being one of the most successful owners in British racing history, John spent 15 years as Liberal MP for South Durham before abandoning politics to enjoy the cultural, artistic and social life of Paris.

Barnard Castle

Dealing in the unexpected was something of a family speciality for the Bowes clan. They left a legacy of an 18th Century estate at Gibside, complete with embellishments such as the original Statue of Liberty, just a short hop from Gateshead MetroCentre.

Left: Barnard Castle, once the stronghold of the Baliol family.

Barnard Castle has been recognised as one of the 51 most historically and architecturally important towns in Britain.

The present-day Galgate is on the line of a Roman road which crossed the River Tees, which flows past the town.

But it was the 12th Century castle, founded by Bernard Baliol, which named the settlement.

For 200 years the castle, which is built on a cliff above the river, was the main stronghold of the Baliol family, who turned it into one of the biggest fortresses in northern England.

John de Baliol owned the castle in the 13th Century and, through his marriage to Devorguilla of Galloway, he became one of the wealthiest men in Britain. When he died in 1269 Devorguilla, who was devoted to his memory, founded Sweetheart Abbey in Dumfries and kept his embalmed heart in a casket throughout her widowhood.

The castle eventually passed into the ownership of Richard III and was later besieged by 5,000 rebels in 1569 during the Rising of the North. Today the dramatic ruins and their sensory garden, look out over the Tees and are in the care of English Heritage.

In 1852 they married and as a wedding present John gave Josephine a chateau which Louis XV had once given to his mistress. Josephine was a painter as well as an actress and her love of the arts was shared by John. This led to the astonishing decision to create a great mansion which would bring a flavour of France to the northern English market town near Streatlam. They bought land on the edge of Barnard Castle and built the French chateau which is now the Bowes Museum. When work on the museum began, John was 50 and Josephine 36. They set themselves the enormous task of filling the huge building with items and spent the next 12 years buying 15,000 objects.

This passion for collecting ended with the death of Josephine, aged 48, in 1874. John died in 1885 without seeing the completion of the building, which opened to the public in 1892.

The Grade I listed museum was eventually taken over by Durham County Council and is now a

Not content with enjoying the stage, John bought the Theatre de Varieties in Paris and took up with the actress Benoite-Josephine Coffin-Chevallier. She was installed with John's support at quarters which would one day house the French Rugby Federation.

Clockwise from top: The Bowes Museum. The Silver Swan. Josephine Bowes. John Bowes.

One of the Bowes Museum's best known exhibits is its Silver Swan. The 230-year-old musical automaton was acquired in 1872 and continues to play every day to visitors at 12.30pm and 3.30pm. Specialist Ray Mand has looked after the Swan for 25 years.

He said: "The Swan is a mechanical marvel and is a privilege to work on."

The intricate mechanical works are believed to be the handiwork of inventor John Joseph Merlin. They were made in the late 18th Century, in the workshop of James Cox, a London Goldsmith.

The Swan is a lifesize model and is controlled by three separate clockwork mechanisms. When set in motion, the Swan appears to preen itself and then bends its neck to take a small fish from the water – which is actually cunningly concealed within its beak.

The Silver Swan was exhibited by the jeweller Harry Emmanuel at the 1867 Paris International Exhibition, which is where John and Josephine Bowes first saw it. The couple purchased the unique automaton five years later for 5000 francs (about £200).

registered charity run by
trustees. It is home to an
array of European art,
furniture, ceramics, Sevres
porcelain, and textiles
spanning 500 years and
paintings which include
works by Canaletto and
Goya.

Just opened is the John
and Josephine gallery,
which tells their story, and
the museum has also
recently acquired the Lady
Ludlow collection of 500
pieces of some of the most
outstanding examples of
18th Century English
porcelain.

There are 23 acres of
grounds for visitors to
enjoy, including a new tree
trail.

But a lasting impression is
the stroll down Galgate
and Horsemarket in
Barnard Castle, with its
17th, 18th and 19th
Century buildings, and
minutes later being in the
middle of a Loire-like
experience on the steps of
the chateau.

The juxtaposition of two
worlds takes some doing.

There are more historic
treats just outside Barnard
Castle. Bowes Castle was
built in the 12th Century on
part of the site of the Roman
fort of Lavatrae. Today, the
keep of the castle survives
overlooking the Greta valley.

Also nearby is Egglestone
Abbey, founded in 1159 and
which struggled against
Scottish raiding parties.

After attacks in 1315 the
abbey's losses were so great
that its tax to the Crown was
halved.

Stone from the abbey was
used at Rokeby Hall, three
miles east of Barnard Castle.
Rokeby Park country house
was the setting for Walter
Scott's ballad, Rokeby.

The Bowes Museum is open daily from 11am-5pm. Admission
is Adults £7, Concessions £6, under-16s free.

Access to the gift shop, café and the park is free. Telephone
01833 690 606.

The castle at Barnard Castle is open from 10am-6pm, April 1-
September 30, October 10am-5pm and Nov – March 10am-
4pm. Admission Adult £3, Concession £2.60, and Children
£1.50. Telephone 01833 638 212.

Egglestone Abbey and Bowes Castle are also both in the care
of English Heritage an entry is free.

Egglestone Abbey is a mile south of Barnard Castle off the
B6277. Bowes Castle is four miles west of the town.

Rokeby Park is three miles east of Barnard Castle and is open
from the end of May on Mondays and Tuesdays from 2pm-
5pm. Admission adults £5, childrren£2.

Telephone 01833 637 334.

The Roman remains at Vindolanda

Vindolanda

Time travel is a favourite province of science fiction, with the fascinating concept of rolling back the centuries and making contact with people from another age the stuff of any number of books and films.

But a particularly beautiful part of Northumberland offers the nearest any of us will get to fulfilling the fantasy.

Since 1973, around 1,700 Latin writing tablets have been unearthed among the superbly-preserved finds pouring from Vindolanda Roman fort. The Vindolanda tablets offer an unprecedented window on the lives and concerns of Vindolanda's people.

They include the 1,000-strong Ninth Cohort of Batavians from Holland, who were the garrison from AD90 to 115 when they left to join Trajan's army on the Danube, the First Cohort of Tungrians from Belgium and the 500-strong Fourth Cohort of Gauls from France.

Outside the fort walls was a substantial civilian settlement of wives and children, merchants, priests and slaves.

From the tablets – the largest collection of original Roman letters ever found – more than 400 individuals emerge from the mists of time. The letters are lodged with the British Museum, and were voted by a panel of experts as the country's greatest treasure in a TV series which examined the finest of finds.

Dr Jeremy Hill, curator at the British Museum, said: "There is virtually no writing from Roman Britain, and the tablets offer a unique insight into life at that time in the form of little postcards from people living in what is now Northumberland."

The letters and documents include:

"..the Britons are unprotected by armour. There are very many cavalry. The cavalry do not use swords, nor do the wretched Britons mount in order to throw javelins."

"while writing this to you, I was making the bed warm."

Vindolanda commander Flavius Cerialis and his wife Sulpicia Lepidina were close friends with Brocchus and his wife Claudia Severa, who were stationed at another fort called Briga. Claudia addresses her friend as "dearest sister" and "longed for soul."

Cerialis talks of the "summers, even if they are unpleasant."

A man who describes himself as being from overseas complains to authority that "I implore you to not allow me, an innocent person, to be beaten with rods."

Above left: The reconstructed temple at Vindolanda.

Above right: Vindolanda Museum where many of the archaeological finds are displayed.

Dr Ralph Jackson, curator of the Vindolanda material at the British Museum, said: "The Vindolanda tablets are simply incomparable. They are the oldest handwritten documents in Britain and are the greatest treasure we possess. They enable us to hear the thoughts of people from so long ago, and that is very exceptional."

Yet the tablets are only a small part of the riches which have emerged from 36 years of annual digs at a site which carries an overwhelming aura of history and the presence of those who settled there across the centuries.

The first fort was built alongside the Roman Stanegate road, about 40 years before work began on Hadrian's Wall.

There have been between eight and 10 forts on the site, which is fed by streams and springs and

Above: Some of the exhibits in the Vindolanda Museum.

Right: Vindolanda writing tablets.

Vindolanda's museum houses a treasure chest of discoveries.

There is jewellery and glass – with one piece decorated by gladiatorial scenes – bronze items, armour, weapons, locks, keys and tools.

A helmet crest has been made from hair moss and is believed to be the only item of its type from Roman times. Also created from hair moss, which had the properties of deterring insects, especially midges, is a lady's wig or hair piece.

Textiles include a child's sock and among the leather footwear of all kinds is an expensive sandal which is thought to have belonged to Sulpicia Lepidina, the wife of Batavian commander Flavius Cerialis.

Amid the remains of his house was found a decorated chamfron, or horse's ceremonial face mask.

Large quantities of clay tiles were recovered from a bath house excavation. When they had been left out to dry, animals had walked over them. More than 300 prints have been identified from dogs, cats, pigs, cattle, sheep and goats.

One ditch contained what can only be described as an essay in disappointment.

The treat of a barrel of oysters, mostly unopened, had been discarded, presumably because they were found to be unfit to eat. Thrown away with the oysters was beautiful and unused red Samian ware pottery, imported from France, which had been damaged in transit. One can imagine the angst as the crate was opened to reveal the high quality goods to be cracked and useless.

shelters under Barcombe Hill. As each fort was levelled, a layer of clay was applied to provide a base for the new buildings, and they have sealed objects in near-perfect conditions for preservation.

So far there have been up to 20,000 leather finds, 2,000 wooden objects, and 9,000 "small finds" such as jewellery, weapons and tools. The total number of finds is approaching 50,000 and director of excavations Robin Birley estimates there are at least 150 years of digging left at Vindolanda. And a recent land acquisition has doubled the area for exploration.

Robin said: "Vindolanda is one of the most exciting archaeological sites in Europe because of the extraordinary degree of preservation. Many finds are better preserved than in Pompeii."

Patricia Birley is director of the Vindolanda Trust, which runs the site and relies mostly on visitor income and its own efforts for funding.

She said: "We feel very much in touch with those who have lived here before. They are real, they had lives and they had personalities.

"The site has its own atmosphere. It is like an natural arena. You feel as if you are enclosed and protected by the landscape."

Such is the site's presence that the trust has regular requests to scatter people's ashes.

Excavated and displayed features include a headquarters building, commander's house, temple, bath house, civilian houses and shops.

Because of Border warfare, Vindolanda was deserted for centuries until the 17th Century when crofters and smallholders drifted back.

An 18th Century croft has been recreated, which shows that the inhabitants endured worse housing and facilities than did the site's Third Century civilians.

But life at Roman Vindolanda was not just about shops and bathing. On show is the skull of a man who had suffered what was probably a spear thrust to the head.

Cemeteries around the

On the approach to Vindolanda is Causeway House, the only dwelling in Northumberland still thatched in heather.

It survived because the 18th Century farmhouse was later used as a store and its thatch was preserved under corrugated iron.

Two 19th Century dresses were found, stuffed into holes in the roof.

The building is now run as a holiday cottage by the Landmark Trust.

fort, which have not been touched, are the last resting place for an estimated 30,000 people.

All life and death is at Vindolanda. Yet one of the most evocative features is a tall Roman milestone, still standing where it was first erected alongside the Stanegate next to the fort.

What times, and how many people passing by, has it witnessed?

Vindolanda is near Bardon Mill, and can be reached from the A69 or the much more atmospheric B6318.

From April to September it is open from 10am-6pm and 5pm at other times.

Admission is £4.50 adults, £3.80 OAPs and students, £2.90 Child, £13 family ticket, under-fives free.

Telephone (01434) 344277. website www.vindolanda.com

The museum has a café and the Twice Brewed pub is nearby, as is the Northumberland National Park Once Brewed visitor centre.

Cragside

June at Cragside in Northumberland and many of the annual 160,000 visitors roll up to enjoy the mass flowering of the estate's forest of rhododendrons.

Left: Cragside formal gardens and the Clock Tower.

Right: Cragside has 55 varieties of rhododendron in the grounds.

This is where the 19th Century inventor Lord Armstrong, who ran an industrial empire on Tyneside which eventually employed 25,000 people, established a country mansion on the edge of Rothbury. He surrounded it with 1,700 acres of wooded pleasure grounds and a series of lakes.

Today the house at Cragside, the first in the world to be lit by hydro-electricity, and 1,000 acres are run by the National Trust. It was also the first house to have modern lamps, using the incandescent bulb invented by Armstrong's friend, Joseph Swan.

House, woodlands, lakes and gardens make for a popular mix and that they are there to be enjoyed today springs from the regular trips the young William Armstrong made with his parents from Tyneside to stay with friends in Rothbury.

The seeds of Cragside were planted during William's boyhood paddling in the River Coquet and climbing on the crags. He suffered from chest complaints and recalled: "More than once an apparently incurable cough was quickly removed by coming to Rothbury and had it not

Clockwise: Cragside House and bridge; Cragside's Drawing Room with its magnificent Italian marble fireplace; the lavish interior at Cragside; the first electric lamp at Cragside.

been for its curative effect there would have been no Cragside."

William also delighted in fishing and was fond of the glen through which the Debdon Burn flowed into the river. Years later he would buy as much of the Debdon valley as he could on his way to creating Cragside.

He continued visiting the area to fish during his early married life and wrote to his wife Margaret in 1843: "I have been almost continuously in the water

this glorious day and there is nothing does me so much good."

It was as well that he took such relaxing breaks at that time. Four years later he set up his works in Elswick in Newcastle, making a wide range of engineering goods but especially the Armstrong hydraulic crane. His enterprise went on to turn out everything from his breech-loading, shell-firing artillery guns to warships.

More than half of the Japanese ironclad ships

A dedicated band of 40 volunteers weighs in regularly to help out at Cragside.

They staff the rooms in the house as security and to talk to visitors, while some lead parties of schoolchildren who come to study Victorian times.

A team is constantly engaged in cleaning the 10,000 books at Cragside, while others trap bugs like carpet beetles or inspect and record fabrics, clothing and ceramics for Cragside's database.

Volunteer and retired librarian Doug Bond says: "We all love Cragside. You fall in love with the place and want to help out.

"It is a wonderful place with a fascinating house and magnificent estate. It is a joy."

Grand though the mansion at Cragside is, it was not Lord Armstrong's only preoccupation.

On a bare, rocky hillside he and his wife Margaret masterminded the planting of seven million trees and shrubs.

Forty miles of paths and steps and a six-mile carriage drive were fashioned. At that time the taste was to imitate foreign landscapes, such as the rhododendron forests of the Himalayas.

Armstrong imported many rhododendrons and azaleas. There are currently 55 varieties of rhododendron and 35 of azalea at Cragside. A labyrinth has been carved from the living rhododendrons which can take the visitor more than an hour to explore.

The intrepid British plant collectors of the day brought back not just rhododendrons from the East but also conifers from North America. Cragside's Pinetum holds a fine collection of conifers, mainly from North America and features England's tallest Douglas Fir.

Another fashion was for rock gardens and the Armstrongs had plenty of raw material with which to work. They went on to build one of the biggest hand-made rock gardens in Europe.

The gardens had become cloaked by ground-creeping shrubs and over the last 15 years four acres have been cleared and restored with another acre to go.

The Armstrongs created their formal garden on fields overlooking the Coquet Valley and its richer soil allowed a range of hardy and tender plants to be cultivated. The gardens include the Clock Tower, which regulated starting, finishing and meal times on the estate, the loggia and the Orchard House.

Restoration of the 1870s Orchard House began in 1992. It was built to grow fruit in earthenware pots sitting on sandstone terraces. Today the Orchard House is used to grow figs, peaches, nectarines, grapes, apples, pears, apricots, plums, gages, grapefruit, oranges and lemons. All the fruit goes to Cragside's restaurant.

The art of carpet bedding has also been revived with each of two beds using 10,000 plants grown in the estate's nursery. The Dahlia Walk has also made a comeback and restoration started four years ago of the Italian Terrace,

The cast iron loggia with its glazed roof and sides was where the Armstrongs would sit to enjoy the view of the Simonside Hills.

Head gardener Andrew Sawyer says: "The views from the garden across the valley are spectacular. It is just magical.

"In the garden we are trying to keep the spirit of the age and the character of the period."

In June around 26,000 visitors are expected – most come to see the rhododendrons.

"They are still the traditional draw but the formal garden is really increasing our visitor numbers when it is at its peak from August to October," says Andrew.

One notable difference between Lord Armstrong's time and now is that he had 70 gardeners. Today there are four, with some seasonal help.

used in the war against Russia in 1905 were Armstrong vessels.

Amid such a hectic schedule, Armstrong made do with naps on a camp bed in his office and largely did without holidays.

But by the early 1860s he became less involved with the day to day running of the company and had begun to look towards returning to the scene of his boyhood excursions. Work began on Cragside in 1863 when Armstrong was 52.

It was to be something of a larger version of his home in Newcastle where he and Margaret had planted and landscaped what is now Jesmond Dene, which the couple gave to the city.

Having bought an initial 20 acres in the Debdon valley, he built a small house which took its name from nearby Cragend Hill. In 1869, Armstrong called in architect Norman Shaw to greatly extend the house, which he did over the next 15 years to produce the fascinating assemblage we see today.

© NTPL/Ian Shaw.

Nelly's Moss Lake.

Visitors follow in the footsteps of the Prince of Wales, who stayed in 1884, the King of Siam, the Shah of Persia and the Crown Prince of Afghanistan. For the Prince of Wales's visit, 10,000 small glass lamps were distributed along the rocky hillside and almost the same number of Chinese lanterns were swung across the leafy glades. Inside, the house blazed with electric light. The light was one example of how Armstrong brought his inventiveness to bear at Cragside.

It was a family saying that Armstrong had "water on the brain." His absorption with hydraulic water power saw him create a system which pumped supplies to turn the kitchen spit, operate a lift, laundry equipment, a sawmill, farm machinery and a dynamo to produce electric light.

Armstrong dammed the burn to form Tumbleton lake, which fed a hydraulic ram to pump water to the gardens and also to a tank at the house for domestic use.

By 1878 the house was using a turbine-powered electric arc lamp and in 1880 it had Swan's incandescent carbon filament light

Armstrong also built the Debdon and Nelly's Moss lakes - now a picturesque feature of the estate - to increase water power at Cragside. The lakes are 340ft above the Power House, built for a turbine and dynamo and which were in use until 1945.

Armstrong filled Cragside with paintings and his collections of stuffed birds, butterflies, shells and the finest of fabrics.

The kitchen had a primitive type of dishwasher and in the dining room the stone inglenook fireplace was adorned with the legend "East or West, Hame's Best," where Armstrong was painted sitting by his Tyneside artist friend H H Emmerson.

Guests were summoned to meals by electric gongs.

The drawing room features a 10-ton beautifully carved marble chimney piece.

Turf was burned in the fireplace, with the smoke being drawn underground to escape from a chimney disguised as a rock pile high up on the hillside.

Cragside is a delightful and very large box of tricks. Not for nothing was it known in its time as the palace of the modern magician.

Cragside is reached via the B6341 off the A697, a mile north of Rothbury or from the south of Rothbury via the B6344 also off the A697.

Cragside is closed on Mondays except for Bank Holidays. The estate stables visitor centre has a shop, restaurant, with optional open courtyard area, and information room. It is open from March 22-October 30 10.30am-5.30pm and from November 2-December 18 Wednesday-Sunday 11am-4pm.

House from March 22-September 25, Tuesday to Sunday, 1pm-5.30pm. September 28-October 31 1pm-4.30pm.

Gardens and estate from March 22-October 30, Tuesday-Sunday 10.30am-7pm. November 2-December 18, Wednesday-Sunday 11am-4pm.

Admission for house, gardens and estate is adult £8.50, child 5-17 £4, family £20 groups £7

Gardens and estate only is £5.70, £2.60 and £14.

Telephone 01669 620 333.

Lindisfarne Priory founded by St Aidan in 635.

Lindisfarne

Cross the causeway to Holy Island off Northumberland and the sensation is that of entering a different world. You are, after all, following in the footsteps of saints, kings and countless pilgrims.

Dunes at Lindisfarne.

It was one of the holiest Anglo-Saxon sites in England and a hugely important early centre of Christianity, winning international recognition as the home of learning and culture.

After St Cuthbert's body was found undecayed in 698 after 11 years of burial and enshrined in the island's St Peter's Church, Lindisfarne became a centre for pilgrimage – and it is still.

Another landmark is the castle, perched on Beblowe Crag - a 90ft cone of rock rising from the pasture land. Facing it is a walled garden created by one of the country's best garden designers, Gertrude Jekyll. Then there is Lindisfarne

In silhouette a statue of St Aidan with Lindisfarne Castle in the background.

Lindisfarne off Northumberland is a spectacular gathering place for birdlife. The food-rich mud and sand flats around Holy Island and Budle Bay are the most extensive in the North-East.

They have been designated a national nature reserve covering 8,535 acres and managed by English Nature. The reserve includes a stretch of the Northumberland Coast Area of Outstanding Natural Beauty.

Lindisfarne is also a Special Protection Area and a Ramsar site wetland of international importance for birds.

The area hosts up to 50,000 waterfowl in winter with a total of 312 species of birds recorded – more than for any other similarly-sized part of Northumberland.

Thrusting out into the North Sea, the island provides a landfall for many migrating birds. It is on the main migration route for millions of birds from Scandinavia and Siberia to Africa and the Mediterranean.

Of the 393 species so far recorded in Northumberland, 32 have made their first appearance on the island or the adjacent national nature reserve. Around 40 species also regularly breed on the island and, as a result,it is a magnet for birders from all over the country.

Autumn signals the start of the arrival of six internationally-important species of wildfowl and wading birds which will over-winter in the area. For the pale-bellied brent geese from Spitzbergen, the reserve is their only regular wintering place in Britain. The other five species are pinkfooted and greylag geese, wigeon, grey plover and bar-tailed godwit.

Autumn onwards also sees the arrival of birds like lapwing, curlew and dunlin.

Upturned boats on the island shore are a reminder of the herring fishing industry. But today most of the fishing is done by cormorants and terns, or gannets which put on a spectacular show with their headlong dive-bombing technique, while eider duck enjoy the local shellfish.

The island dunes support early forget-me-nots, which need little water. In early summer, purple northern marsh orchids flourish along with the pinker early marsh orchid. In July, marsh helleborines flower by the thousand. White-flowered scurvy grass, which once provided vitamins for sailors, grows on the island.

Washed up on the shore are St Cuthbert's beads – the fossilised remains of animals called crinoids, which resemble the broken beads of a rosary.

The dunes and grassland, with plants like Grass of Parnassus, are habitats for dark green fritillary and grayling butterflies, woolly bear tiger moth caterpillars, and the red and green cinnabar moth.

A garden inspired by the Lindisfarne Gospels has been recreated on the island. The garden, by Stan Timmins, made its debut at Chelsea Flower Show where it drew high praise. The garden includes a 12ft Celtic cross and four Canon Tables creating a screen, each representing one of the four evangelists, Matthew, Mark, Luke and John. Stan, who lives in Newcastle, collaborated with the British Library on the garden design. It won a silver award and also featured on BBC TV's Songs of Praise programme. Now the garden occupies a plot opposite the island heritage centre.

national nature reserve, which supports tens of thousands of birds.

The spiritual centre of the island is Lindisfarne Priory. Founded in 635 by St Aidan, it is where the Lindisfarne Gospels and other treasures were created by the monks. The priory's remains which visitors see today date from the 12th Century and stand beside the mainly 13th century Church of St Mary the Virgin, the oldest building in use on the island and which contains Anglo-Saxon stonework. St Aidan was invited by King Oswald of Northumbria to be a missionary bishop, and he chose the island as the home for his community in 635, going on to oversee the establishment of Christianity in the kingdom. Aidan came from the island monastery of Iona off the west coast of Scotland and another island base would have had a natural appeal.

Lindisfarne's pre-eminence was confirmed by St Cuthbert, who became prior and withdrew to live the life of a hermit on Inner Farne. In 685 Cuthbert was elected bishop and on his death in 687 his body was buried in St Peter's Church. When monks exhumed it 11 years later, they expected to find bones which could be enshrined in a casket. But the body was intact. It was placed in a wooden coffin, parts of which still survive.

The Lindisfarne Gospels are believed to have been created for St Cuthbert's enshrinement. They were worked on by a scribe, Eadfrith, who became bishop. St Cuthbert's shrine established Lindisfarne as a pilgrimage centre and that in turn attracted gifts of money, treasures and land. The growing wealth of Lindisfarne also caught the attention of less welcome visitors – the Vikings.

In 793, their raids devastated the island. A stone grave marker in the priory museum bears a carving of a procession of armed warriors, who could be Viking raiders. The monks were forced to leave the island, bearing the body of St Cuthbert and finally reached Durham. This led to the building of one of the greatest cathedrals in Europe, where St Cuthbert is buried. It was from Durham that monks returned to Lindisfarne to build their new priory. Its design reflects that of Durham Cathedral and it is believed that it was in fact built by the same masons.

Today, the surviving rainbow arch of the priory presents one of the island's most dramatic images.

A community trust runs the island's heritage centre. The Lindisfarne Heritage Centre and Museum of Island Life features an exhibition on the creation of the Lindisfarne Gospels. It includes a virtual reality Turning the Pages screen version of the Gospels and a facsimile copy from the British Library.

Other touch-screen facilities cover scenes on the island with matching text and island folk who talk about their lives.

The centre is managed by the Holy Island of Lindisfarne Community Development Trust.

Centre manager Gillian Douglas has lived on the island for almost 30 years.

She says: "I don't think people realise how much is here and that there is also a living community on the island.

"It is a lovely place and a special place.

"If you love it when you first visit, you will come back year after year."

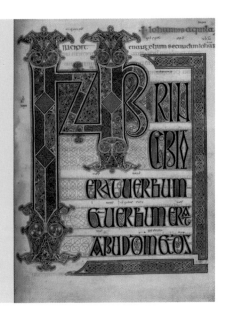

A complex of monastic buildings stands next to the priory. They include remains of what was probably the 13th Century infirmary, the warming house - originally the only room where a fire was allowed - the prior's lodging, brewhouse, bakehouse kitchen and guest accommodation.

The priory suffered in the Anglo-Scottish wars and in the 14th Century the church was fortified. In 1537, Henry VIII's commissioners closed it and it seems to have been disused by the 17th Century, having served as a storehouse as Lindisfarne became part of the Crown's border defences.

The great and the good have passed through, or lived on, Lindisfarne, among a procession of people over the centuries attracted by this alluring island. Among them are two who left a tantalising trace of their lives.

One of its earliest stone carvings is a grave marker from about 1,300 years ago to an individual called Osgyd. Outside the museum, in the churchyard, is a gravestone which has lost most of its inscription, apart from the name - Field Flowers. It is a name which is at one with its setting.

Lindisfarne can only be reached at low tide. There are tide tables at each end of the causeway. The tide times are also carried in local newspapers or can be had from Berwick tourist information centre on (01289) 330 733.

Lindisfarne Priory and its newly-refurbished museum, which are in the care of English Heritage, is open from March 24-September 30 daily from 9.30am-5pm and 9.30am-4pm during October. November 1-March 31 Monday, Saturday and Sunday from 10am-2pm.

Closed 24-26 December and 1 January.

Admission: adults £3.60, concessions £2.70, children £1.80.

Telephone (01289) 389 200.

Lindisfarne National Nature Reserve: Tel (01289) 381 470.

Lindisfarne Heritage Centre and Museum of Island Life is open daily from April 1-end of October 10am-5pm and 10am-4pm in winter.

Admission is £2.50 adults and children under 15 free when accompanied by adult.

Tel: (01289) 389004.

Lindisfarne Castle

The trio who travelled by train from London to the island of Lindisfarne off Northumberland were a trifle unusual, to say the least. The party included Gertrude Jekyll, one of Britain's greatest garden designers, who had brought a large bag of peppermint bullseye sweets to sustain her during the journey. She was accompanied by the architect Sir Edwin Lutyens, who went on to design more than 30 country houses, the Thiepval war memorial arch on the Somme, the Cenotaph in London, the Viceroy's House in New Delhi and the British Embassy in Washington. The third member of the party in 1906 was Black Jack, a raven.

Lindisfarne Castle had been bought by Edward Hudson, London born and bred founder of Country Life magazine, who had decided to sample - at least part-time - the lifestyle his publication embraced. He commissioned Lutyens to create an Edwardian home within the framework of the Tudor castle.

As far as the large black bird was concerned, it earned its passage north because to Lutyens castles meant ravens.

Lindisfarne had, of course, been a great religious centre. But in Tudor times its principal purpose was very different. It became part of the Crown's Border defences and its harbour a base for use against the Scots. The role of the harbour was demonstrated in 1543 when a Royal expedition against the Scots saw 2,000 troops on the island and 10 warships anchored in the haven.

The island's crag was chosen as the site for a stone fortress, built between 1565 and 1571 to protect the harbour, at a cost of more than £1,000.

In her long life from 1843 to 1932, Gertrude Jekyll's reputation was such that she received about 350 garden design commissions in Britain, the United States and across Europe. She often worked with architect Sir Edwin Lutyens, who designed her Munstead Wood home in Surrey.

Her brief at Lindisfarne was to create a walled garden which could be seen from the castle and with the castle forming the backdrop to views from the garden. Her choice of plants included roses, fuchsia, sunflowers, hollyhocks, gladiolus, Japanese anemones, lavatera, godetia, santolina, salvia, campanulas, cornflowers, chrysanthemums, delphiniums, sweet peas, clematis and sedum.

Over the years the garden wandered from Gertrude Jekyll's original plan and planting and in 2002 the National Trust set out to restore it.

This has been the task of trust gardener Philippa Hodkinson, who lives near Wallington in Northumberland. She has worked from the original scheme, which was among a bunch of documents bought in England by an American soldier at a sale during the Second World War. The Jekyll documents are now held at the University of California in Berkeley.

Philippa says: "Edward Hudson would mostly have used the castle during the summer and the original design for the garden included a lot of hardy annuals."

Consequently the garden is at its peak in July. Research has resulted in many of the original varieties of flowers being reintroduced and a vegetable border re-established.

"We were serious about trying to get the right varieties. We felt that if we were going to do it, we would do it properly," says Philippa.

"Gertrude Jekyll was a fantastic designer with a really good eye, and the garden is full of scent, especially from the sweet peas and the roses.

"On a hot day you can smell the garden before you reach it. It has been really good to see her original plans come back to life and hopefully the garden will get better and better."

It was garrisoned until 1819 and later reused as a coastguard station. A second fortification, Osborne's Fort, was built near the priory and the foundations of the redoubt and traces of the perimeter wall remain.

But the neglected Lindisfarne castle was gifted a new life when in 1901 Hudson came across the site and decided it was just the ticket for a holiday home.

"I want to amuse myself with the place," he wrote.

Lutyens introduced interiors linked by dramatic corridors, galleries and stairways, and employed whitewashed walls, patterned brick floors, brass, blue and white china and sturdy furniture. Both Hudson and Lutyens were admirers of 17th century Dutch culture and a series of photographs was commissioned of the architect's children in the castle to echo the feel of the Dutch painter Vermeer's works.

Hudson's new home attracted an array of guests to the island, including the future King George V and Queen Mary, ballerina Alicia Markova and conductor Malcolm Sargent.

The first feature which would have caught their attention is a wind indicator in the entrance hall of Hudson's castle.

It is operated by a weather vane on top of the castle and at its centre is a map of the island and around that a painting of the Spanish Armada being pursued by the English fleet across the North Sea and past Lindisfarne.

Lutyens created two of the main rooms - the dining room and Ship Room - from the castle's gunpowder magazines and both have vaulted roofs to take the weight of the cannons sited in the

Lindisfarne Castle Garden.

battery above. The Ship Room takes its name from a model of the 1840s sailing ship the Henrietta, which is suspended from the ceiling.

In the Upper Gallery, a cello is a reminder that the room was used by Hudson's cellist friend Madame Suggia, who played Bach suites for hours on a Stradivarius which Hudson gave her.

From the Upper Battery of the castle there are sweeping views across to the Farne Islands, Bamburgh Castle, Ross Sands and Fenham Sands.

In addition to the VIPs who visited the castle, Billy Congreve was a guest for two months. He was the youngest son of Hudson's friend General Sir Walter Congreve, who had won the VC in the Boer War and his wife Celia la Touche, who was to be awarded the Croix de Guerre for her nursing work on the Western Front in the First World War. Billy stayed on Lindisfarne to recover from diphtheria, and was a favourite of Hudson, who planned to leave the castle to him. But in the First World War Billy, who had won the MC and the DSO, was killed on the Somme in July, 1916, while tending the wounded under heavy fire. He was awarded a posthumous VC – the first soldier to have won all three medals for gallantry.

Hudson sold the castle in 1921 for £11,000 to stockbroker Oswald Falk, who in turn parted with it to merchant banker Sir Edward de Stein. He gave it to the National Trust but remained its tenant until he died in 1965.

It was in that year that the castle was the setting for Roman Polanski's film Cul-de-Sac, starring Donald Pleasance.

That involved one of the most unlikely scenes ever to take place on the island, which involved Donald Pleasance dressed in a nightie and the French actress Francoise Dorleac running naked along the beach on a cold January day.

Lindisfarne Castle is run by the National Trust.

It is open from March 12-October 30 except Monday and February 12-20 daily. Times vary with the tides.

The castle will be open for four and a half hours, which will always include noon-3pm.

Admission is £5, child £2.50, family £12.50.

The garden is open all year round from 10am-5pm. Admission £1, child free.

Teesdale

If any natural feature has the power to mesmerise, it's the waterfall. And you can have your fill of waterfalls in Teesdale in County Durham.

In Upper Teesdale there is Cauldron Snout, a short way down the valley the thundering power of High Force, then Low Force and Summerhill Force. They are part of a fascinating mix in an area of valley bottom dale hay meadows and whitewashed farmhouses and wild upland which is part of the second biggest national nature reserve in England.

It is raw country around Cow Green in Upper Teesdale, a reservoir which was completed in 1971 amid huge controversy and a battle by conservationists to prevent its construction. One of their main objections was the loss of 20pc of an area which is home to rare alpine plants such as spring gentian - found on the UK mainland only in Teesdale - mountain pansy and yellow marsh saxifrage. These plants originally colonised the high Pennines after the last Ice Age. Elsewhere they have been ousted by more competitive plants, but in Upper Teesdale soil and climate conditions, plus low grazing levels, have allowed them to survive.

Beyond Cow Green lie the high summits of the North Pennines. The view takes in Mickle Fell, Meldon Hill, Great Dunn Fell, Little Dun Fell and Cross Fell - the highest point of the Pennine range.

At the base of the reservoir is Cauldron Snout, where the Tees tumbles over the Whin Sill, a very hard band of rock created around 295m years ago when molten quartz dolerite pushed its way to the surface. The rock cooled into six-sided block formations which can be seen further downriver as crags at Falcon Clints and Cronkley Scar.

Opposite: Low Force, Teesdale
Left: High Force, Teesdale

Follow the Tees down the dale and suddenly the river drops 70ft. This is High Force, reputed to be the highest unbroken fall of water in England.

A gentle quarter-mile walk from the main dale road takes visitors to High Force which can be heard long before it comes into sight. High Force is one of the star turns of the Moor House-Upper Teesdale National Nature Reserve which takes in around 18,000 acres of County Durham and Cumbria.

Nowhere else in Britain is there such a diversity of rare habitats in one location. They include hay

After the power of High Force come the more gentle cascades of Low Force. Nearby is Durham Wildlife Trust's Bowlees nature reserve, based around what was once a limestone quarry.

A visitor centre is housed in a former Methodist chapel built in 1845.

A nature trail through the reserve includes small waterfalls and leads to Gibson's Cave.

The cave has been formed by the Summerhill Force

waterfall partly undercutting the limestone behind it.

Tracking down the dale is the picturesque conservation area settlement of Middleton-in-Teesdale, which dates from the 12th Century.

It grew in the 19th Century when lead mining was the boom industry in the North Pennines and the London Lead Company chose Middleton-in-Teesdale as its northern base.

A terrace of cottages,

built in 1849 as part of that expansion, is called California Row because the homes went up in the same year as the Californian Gold Rush.

The Meet the Middletons visitor attraction in Chapel Row, through a family called Middletons, tells the story of the lead mining community.

Next stop is Eggleston Hall Gardens. The four-acre site was the kitchen gardens for the adjacent Egglestone Hall.

Visitors can buy the plants they see in the gardens from the site's nursery. An added treat is coming across the shell of the old parish church within the gardens. It is surrounded by headstones dating from the early 17th Century, and the RSPB has set up nest boxes and feeding stations.

Inside the walls, part of the church has been planted as a surprise garden. The effect is one of perfect peacefulness.

Above: River Tees, Teesdale.

Right: Pastoral views over Middleton, Teesdale.

meadows, the country's biggest juniper woodland, limestone grassland, blanket bogs and upland summit heaths.

A long track record of scientific research means that the reserve is the best understood upland site in the world.

Scientists from the Centre for Ecology and Hydrology are currently investigating the effects of climate change on upland plant and animal communities.

Chris McCarty is English Nature site manager for the reserve and works with wife Heather, who is community liaison officer. The couple, who met at

Durham University, live with children Joe and Claire in the Teesdale village of Newbiggin, which happens to have what is believed to be the world's oldest Methodist chapel still in continuous use. John Wesley preached several times at the chapel, which opened in 1760.

Chris describes how Cow Green reservoir acts as a heat sink in summer, absorbing warmth, and as a radiator in winter. A meteorological station was set up in 1968 to monitor the impact of Cow Green on the local climate.

Chris and Heather delight in the alpine plants and upland nesting birdlife,

such as lapwing, golden plover, black grouse, curlew, redshank, snipe, dunlin and merlin. The reserve is a European Special Protection Area for its birds and a Special Area of Conservation for its other attributes.

"For a single area there are more features of international importance then anywhere else in Britain. That gives you some idea of the scale of its importance," says Chris.

English Nature manages the reserve in co-operation with the Raby and Strathmore estates and local farmers whose more traditional farming style helps the birdlife.

Left: This beautiful waterfall can be found in Bowlees Nature reserve.

Right: Isolated farms in Teesdale.

"Birds such as lapwing have declined by 70pc elsewhere in the country but here we have them in good numbers," says Chris.

Heather leads public bird safaris to give people the chance to find out more about the areas's 10,000 pairs of breeding waders.

She says: "It is the last breeding stronghold in England for waders. Every morning I see lapwing chicks running around and it's sad that it can't be like that in other parts of the country.

"Upper Teesdale is a wonderful and very special place but some people may not realise what a wildlife jewel lies in their midst."

The B6278 from Barnard Castle or the B6277 from Alston runs through Teesdale.

A scenic route from the north is to travel from Gateshead on the B6278 from Shotley Bridge across the moorlands of Muggleswick and Bollihope commons to Middleton-in-Teesdale.

There is a car park at Cow Green and an easy round-trip three-mile walk to Cauldron Snout. The walk takes in the plants, birdlife and geology which make the area special.

The best time to see both plants and birds is May-July.

English Nature has produced leaflet guides for the walk. Ring 01661 845 500.

The car park at High Force is off the B6277. There is a charge of £1.50 and admission to the falls is £1 adults and 50p children.

The High Force Hotel is a free house. There is also a gift shop, WCs and picnic area.

Bowless nature reserve was WCs, picnic area and the visitor centre has a small shop. Telephone 01833 622 292.

Newbiggin Chapel is open every Wednesday from 2pm-4.30pm until the end of August.

Egglestone Hall Gardens and nursery is open from 10am-5pm daily. Admission to the gardens is £1.

There is also a bistro and shop. Telephone 01833 650 115.

Meet the Middletons is open daily 11am-5pm. There is an admission charge. Telephone 01833 640 333.

An aerial view of Warkworth Castle

Warkworth

The Northumbrian coast is one of the North-East's great showpieces.

Its quality is such that it has amassed an array of designations. From Amble to Berwick it is an Area of Outstanding Natural Beauty and from Alnmouth to St Abb's Head, a European Marine Site.

In 1973, it was one of the first areas in England to be given Heritage Coast status. It also includes sites of special scientific interest, national nature reserves and European Special Protection Areas.

At the southern end of this superb stretch is the estuary of one of the county's finest waterways - the River Coquet.

And Warkworth Castle. Approaching Warkworth from the north offers, according to the architectural critic Nikolaus Pevsner, one of the most exciting sequences of views in England.

First there is the 14th Century fortified bridge - one of the few of its type in the country - then Bridge Street at an angle to join the main street climbing the hill at the top of which looms Warkworth Castle.

The castle is one of the most impressive examples in Britain of an aristocratic fortified residence, and

makes its appearance in Shakespeare's Henry IV.

The charming River Coquet loops around the Warkworth peninsula, with the castle on the high ground and at the other end of the village, the Norman church of St Lawrence.

Settlement at such a prime spot goes back a long way and Warkworth is first recorded in the early 8th Century.

While the village is a delightful mix of old pubs, restaurants, galleries and speciality shops, and regularly excels in the Northumbria in Bloom competition, it is the fortress which dominates - as it was always intended to

Imposing though the castle is, a pleasant stroll along the banks of the River Coquet brings visitors to what is surely Warkworth's greatest surprise and delight.

The walk ends at a crossing point where a rowing boat ferries folk to Warkworth Hermitage, on the far bank. While the castle had chapels, the belief was in times of danger you could not say enough prayers and the hermitage was an extra place of intercession with the Almighty. Hermits, devoted to prayer, were probably supported by the lord of the castle.

The hermitage is remarkable. Two chambers have been cut out of the rock face. In the chapel, columns are carved from the rock and ribbing from the ceiling. There is an altar, a quatrefoil window, a rock basin for the priest to wash his hands and a worn carving of the Nativity.

Above the door leading into the sacristy is a shield carved with instruments of the Passion. The sacristy was where the hermit could store sacred vessels – there are two cupboards cut into the north wall. There is also an altar.

The lord of Warkworth and his household could have joined the hermit in prayer, made confession or heard him preach. By the late 15th Century, the hermit had a yearly allowance of 66 shillings, eight pence (£13.33), as well as pasture for 12 cattle, a bull and two horses. He received 20 loads of firewood a year and fish every Sunday. His garden provided food in what is still a beautiful setting.

There are three miles of sandy beach, backed by dunes, running northwards from Warkworth to Alnmouth.

The stretch is part of a coast which has everything – dunes, castles, sandy bays, rocky reefs, rock pools, boulder shoreline and sheltered mudflats rich in food for birds.

A guide to exploring the shore has been published by the Northumberland Coast Area of Outstanding Natural Beauty Partnership.

The stretch from Amble to Boulmer, which includes Warkworth, is dominated by open sandy beaches which front duneland, with the sand flats of the Aln estuary at the centre.

North of Alnmouth are the intertidal rocky reefs with fine examples at Marden Rocks in Alnmouth Bay and around Seaton Point and Boulmer.

do. It is, in fact, two castles: the huge keep, then the fortifications and towers on the land surrounding this central feature.

The earliest 12th Century fortress appears to have been built by Earl Henry of Northumberland to defend the crossing of the river from the south, with the fortified bridge later protecting against attack from the north.

By 1292 Warkworth Castle was grand enough to welcome Edward I as a guest. In 1332 Edward III granted the castle to Henry de Percy II, the lord of Alnwick, and this began a long link between the fortress and the family.

Although in the care of English Heritage, it is still owned today by the Duke of Northumberland.

The family alternated between Alnwick and Warkworth castles and

Henry de Percy II and III both died in the latter.

Although Warkworth Castle was built to withstand attack, it also represented the power of its owners.

Visitors to the castle would have been impressed by the 13th Century gatehouse.

Passing through the gatehouse, they would have found themselves in an open space surrounded by the Lion, Grey Mare's Tail, Montague, Carrickfergus and West Postern towers, creating a striking effect.

The keep was built in the 14th Century and in the 1850s the Fourth Duke, Algernon Percy, and architect Anthony Salvin drew up plans to restore the great building. Work was completed on only three rooms and they are now open to the public.

The seclusion of a 16-acre island off the River Coquet estuary today offers a refuge to thousands of seabirds.

Coquet Island is home to the entire UK breeding population of roseate terns.

That same seclusion attracted monks of a Benedictine monastery, built there and incorporated into the 19th Century lighthouse.

In 1839 The Journal reported "the lighthouse, so long contemplated on Coquet

Island, is immediately to be built". Bought by the Duke of Northumberland in 1753, the island's tradition as a bird haven was established by his notice proclaiming shooting, trespassing or fishing would merit prosecution.

The island is still owned by the Duke and is managed as a reserve by the RSPB.

Its peace was interrupted in 1643 as it was garrisoned in the Civil War by Royalist troops but calm was restored on their surrender to Scots.

At the turn of the last century, lighthouse keepers' families lived on the island. The only occupants today are seasonal RSPB wardens.

As it is a bird sanctuary, people cannot walk around the island but there are boat tours from Amble.

It is the southernmost breeding spot for eider ducks and is also important for puffins and common terns, Arctic, roseate and sandwich terns.

The spot where St Lawrence's Church now stands in Warkworth has been a religious site for more than 1,200 years.

The Percy family built the south aisle in the 15th Century and the beams of the original lead roof can be seen.

There is Norman stone vaulting in the chancel roof and pieces of ancient crosses are on display, including one example of carved chainwork dating back to the original church.

At 90ft, the nave is the longest Norman nave in Northumberland and the church also has the tomb and effigy of a knight called Sir Hugh, who would have almost certainly been associated with the castle.

Village children were taught in a small room above the porch and in 1819, 60 farmers and gentry subscribed to make it a day school.

It was outside the church that the Old Pretender was first proclaimed king by a rebel force during the Jacobite rebellion of 1715. The night before, one of the rebel leaders, the Earl of Derwentwater, and 40 followers ate in the Masons Arms, which is still dispensing hospitality to diners with less rebellious tendencies.

The Duke hung the rooms with tapestries and leather wall coverings, and furnished them with replica Elizabethan and 17th Century items. Some of the larger furniture pieces could not negotiate the spiral staircase and had to be sawn in half and re-assembled.

The rooms were used by a succession of Dukes to entertain friends on excursions from Alnwick until the rooms were placed under the guardianship of English Heritage in 1987.

Warkworth Castle is open from April 1 until September 30, 10am-6pm daily; October 1 until 31 from 10am-4pm daily; November 1 until March 31 10am-4pm Saturday to Monday.

Admission Adult £3.30, Concession £2.50, Child £1.70, family ticket £8.30.

Tel: (01665) 711 423.

The hermitage is open from April 1 until September 30, 11am-5pm on Wednesdays, Sundays and Bank holidays.

Admission Adult £2.30, Concession £1.70, Child £1.20.

The remains of the Bath House at Chesters fort

Chesters

The abiding feeling is that troops in the Roman Army who hailed from sunnier climes must have felt left out in the cold on Hadrian's Wall on the northernmost frontier of the empire. If that was the case, they would have drawn some compensatory comfort at Chesters fort near Chollerford in Northumberland. The base was occupied for nearly 300 years, with several changes of garrison, including Asturian Spanish cavalry.

In fact, it is the best preserved example of a Roman cavalry fort in Britain.

It sits near the banks of the River North Tyne and enjoys beautiful views which the bath house - itself one of the best preserved in Roman Britain - takes in. Certainly, the patrons of the bath house would have been familiar with the sort of show which nature performed as I paused for 15 minutes on the river edge. As a buzzard circled high overhead, a heron stood still in the river shallows before lunging forward and seizing a good-sized fish. It took off, flipped the fish in mid-air, and swallowed it before landing to try its luck again.

Next came a goosander trailing a flotilla of ducklings, with some hopping on and off her back.

It's a lovely spot, and one which must have been equally appreciated by the 500-strong fort garrison and 19th Century landowner John Clayton.

The fort remains are in parkland laid out by the Clayton family in the early 19th Century and John Clayton himself was a man of astonishing vigour and foresight. He inherited the 18th Century Chesters House next to the fort from his father Nathaniel.

Haven is an overworked word. But if ever it had an accurate application then it is to Chesters Walled Garden, a few minutes' walk from the fort. Susie White has invested 18 years in the two-acre, 18th Century site, which was once the garden of Chesters House.

Woods of beech and yew shelter the garden, which slopes gently south to maximise the sunshine. This all creates a microclimate which supports a range of plants such as eucalyptus and cistus that are not always guaranteed to survive a Northumbrian winter.

The garden has one of the largest collections of herbs in the country, with 900 different species and varieties, including the national thyme and marjoram collections. Centre-stage goes to the 30-metre-long thyme bank, at its best in late June and July, when its Persian carpet display of pinks, purples, whites, gold and silver attract the bees.

The Roman herb garden is divided into four formal beds in a scaled-down version of what Romans would have cultivated in villa courtyards. This is apt as Hadrian's Wall runs 20 yards north of the garden and the line of a Roman road crosses the site at an angle.

The garden displays herbs known to have been grown in Britain during the Roman occupation. They include culinary herbs marjoram, chives, marshmallow, sage, fennel, Good King Henry, mint and rosemary, medicinal herbs such as betony, fig, rue and pennyroyal, and sacred herbs like violets, myrtle, acanthus, lavender and vervain.

There are espalier apple trees more than 100 years old, a Mediterranean border and pond, herbaceous borders and beds, a gold and silver border, circular pool and a re-creation of a 1671 knot garden.

And, not surprisingly, 80 species of birds have been seen in the garden.

Susie, who is also a painter, printmaker and photographer, makes the point that

Above: Susie White in Chesters walled garden.

there is much more to the garden than herbs. She says: "Because it is an organic garden, a lot of the plants have been chosen for the birds, bees and butterflies, with wild flowers placed with rare and exotic specimens.

"I'm not a plant snob and simply choose plants I like."

On the pervasive appeal of the garden, she says: "Walled gardens give a comforting, enclosing feeling and they have a very special and protecting atmosphere.

"It is a very natural looking garden and I get comments from visitors saying how relaxed and at ease they feel."

Clayton, who died in 1890 aged 98, and John spent much of his time excavating Chesters fort and other sites along the central section of Hadrian's Wall. He had seen how stretches of the wall were being pillaged for building stone and over the years acquired five of the major Roman sites in the area to protect them. He took part in his last dig at the age of 94. As well as his one-man archaeological mission, bachelor Clayton was town clerk of Newcastle for 45 years and played a leading role with developer Richard Grainger in creating what is now known as Grainger Town in the city centre. He was also head of one of the biggest law firms in the North-East and clerk to bodies dealing with everything from the management of the Tyne and asylums to roads and lighting.

As well as uncovering areas of Chesters fort, Clayton supervised digs at Housesteads, Carrawburgh and Carvoran.

One of his most spectacular excavations was at the well of Coventina at Carrawburgh. It produced 24 stone altars, most of them dedicated to Coventina, pottery incense burners and around 14,000 Roman coins which are now in the British Museum.

Above: St Oswald's Church.

Shortly before reaching Chesters from the east, a wooden cross stands beside the B6318, known as the Military Road. It was erected in the 1930s to mark the Battle of Heavenfield in 635.

Before the battle against the Celtic King Cadwalla, the Christian King Oswald raised his cross on high ground where St Oswald's Church now stands. Cadwalla was killed on the banks of the Rowley Burn and the victory re-established a Christian King of Northumbria.

A short walk up the slope from the cross takes the visitor to the church, which was rebuilt in 1737.

The first church was built in the late Seventh Century and the spot was a place of pilgrimage for centuries.

Clayton's collection is housed in a museum at English Heritage's Chesters fort and is largely displayed as it was at the turn of the last century. In effect, it is a historical exhibit in itself. Clayton collected so much that 4,000 items are held in a reserve and are not on show. The discovery of old visitor books suggests that the museum was at least partly open in 1896 after being commissioned by Clayton's nephew Nathaniel. It was built at the bottom of the drive to Chesters House.

Very few museums in the country have as many Roman stones bearing inscriptions and sculptures as Chesters.

"They give an immense amount of information about how Hadrian's Wall was built, who built it, officers in the army, units stationed at the fort, and the religions followed by the troops," says Georgina Plowright, English Heritage curator of Hadrian's Wall museums. They include statues of the goddess Juno Dolichena and her consort Jupiter, who were a Third Century cult, and of Neptune reclining, which was found in the fort commander's house. One inscription records the First Cohort of Dalmatians, from the Balkans, and the First Cohort of Vangiones from the Upper Rhineland.

Left: John Clayton

Right: Some of the altars and inscriptions at the museum at Chesters fort.

Another of Clayton's finds, discovered at Carvoran, is a bronze corn holder, which holds 17 pints of grain and is the only one of its type to be found in Britain. It is believed to have been used to measure a soldier's corn ration for a week.

Excavations of the east guardroom of the south gate revealed a diploma dated AD146. This was issued to an auxiliary soldier on his retirement and legalised his marriage and granted him and his children - but not his wife - Roman citizenship. He would no doubt have enjoyed the star attraction at Chesters - the bath house.

The remains include a large changing room and seven alcoves, thought to have contained statues representing days of the week - Sol (the sun), Luna (the moon), Mars, Mercury, Jupiter, Venus and Saturn. A statue of the goddess Fortuna was also found, indicating that gaming went with the bathing. A range of services were on offer. There were the hot dry rooms where charcoal furnaces kept the temperature high, steam heat treatments, cold and hot baths. This was comfort on the frontier indeed.

Clayton, a devotee of the Classics, even called his dog Marcus Aurelius. Georgina says: "He had so much energy. He was a man of great charm and ability who got up at 6am to teach his sister Latin before he went to work."

Chesters Roman fort, run by English Heritage, is near Chollerford, off the B6318.

It has a café, shop and toilets.

Open: April 1-September 30, 9.30am-6pm daily.

October 1- March 31, 10am-4pm daily.

Admission adults £3.60, concessions £2.70, children £1.80.

Telephone (01434) 681 379.

Chesters Walled Garden is a next to the fort. It has a shop and plant sales area.

Open: 10am-5pm daily April-Oct. October 30-March 31 reduced winter opening times. Admission is £2.50, children under 10 free. Admission to plant nursery is free.

Telephone (01434) 681 483.

Bamburgh Castle

It is the North-East's Rock of Ages – an unbeatable combination of natural and man-made grandeur. Bamburgh Castle, sitting on its great mound of volcanic rock facing the sea, is one of the defining sights of the North. The ultimate in natural fortresses, the Northumbrian site has been occupied and defended for 2,000 years.

For many years it was the centre of royal power, adding to its extraordinary presence in the landscape.

In the Iron Age this outcrop of the Whin Sill was likely to have been the defended base of a regional chieftain and the year 547 is the traditional date given for the occupation of Bamburgh by the Anglo-Saxon King Ida.

Bamburgh became the royal citadel of the kings of Bernicia, who eventually absorbed the neighbouring kingdom of Deira. That created the kingdom of Northumbria, and the Venerable Bede suggests that the name of Bamburgh came from Bebba, the wife of King Ida's grandson, Ethelfrith.

The site was called Bebbaburgh, or Bebba's fortress – and it must have been impressive.

For Simeon of Durham wrote in 774: "The city of Bebba is extremely well fortified. It has a church of very beautiful architecture, in which is a shrine. In this, wrapped in a pall, lies the uncorrupted right hand of St Oswald." It was Oswald who was instrumental in setting up a monastery on nearby Lindisfarne in 625.

The Christian king, after triumphing at the Battle of Heavenfield, near Chollerford, in Northumberland in 642 against the Celtic king

Cadwalla, was himself killed in a clash with Penda of Mercia. Oswald's body was hacked to pieces but they were removed from the battlefield by his brother and deposited as relics in churches. His arm is believed to have been placed in the Bamburgh fortress church.

For such an important site, Bamburgh had been the subject of surprisingly little archaeological investigation. Dr Brian Hope-Taylor, who died in 2001, did carry out a series of excavation up to the 1970s, and this is now being built upon.

The Bamburgh Project, which is led by archaeologists Phil Wood, Graeme Young, Paul Gething and Gerry Twomey, carried out a radar

In the grounds of St Aidan's Church is the tomb of Grace Darling, daughter of the keeper of the Longstone lighthouse on the Farne Islands off Bamburgh.

Their heroism in rowing through storm-lashed seas to rescue survivors of the wrecked paddle steamer Forfarshire in 1838 made Grace a national figure. She died in 1842 from consumption, aged 26.

Queen Victoria contributed to a memorial and it was built in 1844 in the churchyard in a position

which could be seen by sailors at sea. By 1885 it had deteriorated and a new figure of Grace was carved from the original model.The original now lies in the nave of the church. The future of the village's Grace Darling museum has been secured with the award of almost £1m in lottery cash.

survey on the church site. It detected what appeared to be an underground vaulted chamber, which could be an Anglo-Saxon crypt used to house the St Oswald relic.

The project has also investigated the well which served the Bamburgh royal household and which still exists today.

At more than 130ft deep, it was found to be an astonishing feat of human labour. The first 66ft was cut through the extremely hard dolerite rock, with the same length being dug through sandstone and smoothly finished.

Graeme Young says: "The well was cut from the

The life of Lord Armstrong, who so dominated Tyneside in the 19th Century and created the Cragside estate in Northumberland, is celebrated in a museum based in what was the castle laundry.

But the building also houses a fascinating collection of pieces from Second World War aircraft, on loan from Derek Walton of Seahouses. These include :

A propellor from a German ME110 or Ju88, netted by fishermen in 1981.

An ME110 main wheel tyre which was washed up at Seahouses in 1998 –

probably from an aircraft shot down on August 15, 1940, by Spitfires from RAF Acklington in Northumberland.

An engine, snared in fishing nets off Blyth in 1989, from a Heinkel HE111 bomber.

Part of the engine from a Dornier D0127 bomber, shot down in 1943.

A tyre from a Dornier brought down in 1942 off Blyth and found by a fishing boat off the port in 1995.

The aircraft parts are relics of warfare 60 years ago – a continuation of conflicts which have swirled around the castle for centuries.

One of the strangest stories to emerge from Bamburgh is that of General Tom Forster. The castle was occupied for some years by the Forster family, latterly by brother and sister Tom and Dorothy, who were in a bad way financially.

Perhaps with an eye on rectifying that situation, Tom joined the Jacobite Rebellion of 1715, and was made a general.

After his surrender, he was imprisoned in London and was visited on several occasions by Dorothy and her maid.

One day Dorothy paid a visit alone, but was wearing her maid's clothing under her own. She dressed Tom in the maid's clothes and the guards, used to seeing two women leave the cell, suspected nothing.

All three fled back to Bamburgh, where Dorothy hid Tom for two years. He eventually escaped to France by ship from nearby Waren Burn.

highest point of the rock and must rate as a remarkable piece of Northumbrian engineering. This represents a remarkable technical achievement and an immense human effort, reflecting the importance that a secure water supply held for the defence of a fortress."

Dr Hope-Taylor's dig in 1971 unearthed along with 70 Anglian coins and a sword, a small gold plaque engraved with a creature later called the Bamburgh Beast.

In 1894, construction work uncovered layers of what is believed to have been kitchen waste in a hollow in the rock.

The layers included an early 9th Century styca coin and the bones of ox, sheep, pig, deer, and the shells of oyster, mussel, limpet, and periwinkle which gives an insight into the diet of those who lived in the citadel at that time.

One of the major Bamburgh finds came in the 19th Century, when a carved stone piece was discovered as undergrowth was cleared. For years it was thought to be part of an Anglo-Saxon cross but Prof Rosemary Cramp from Durham University re-examined the stone and identified it as a section of the arm of a chair, which could have been the throne of the kings of Northumbria.

The Normans took over the Bamburgh site. A mighty keep was built in the 12th Century and survives reasonably intact. During the medieval period, Bamburgh developed as a sophisticated castle.

Among the kings who stayed at Bamburgh were John, Henry III, and Edward I, II and III.

In 1328 the castle resisted a three-month Scottish siege and two more in

Above: The Bamburgh Castle burial ground.

Right: The Bamburgh Castle dig.

1333 and 1346. But it could not cope with the evolution of artillery and was badly damaged by cannon fire in 1462 in a 14-day Wars of the Roses siege.

Bamburgh was, in fact, the first castle in England to fall to artillery fire.

In 1704 it was bought by Nathaniel, Lord Crewe, the last of the Prince Bishops of Durham.

At the end of the 19th Century its owner was the Tyneside industrialist and inventor Lord Armstrong and he began the reconstruction of the castle as a grand residence. Today, the castle is still the home of the Armstrong family and its spectacular setting attracts 100,000 visitors a year.

Storms – as the Grace Darling legend attests – have always lashed the Bamburgh coastline. Today the castle is separated from the sea by dunes and a superb beach.

But some 18th and 19th Century paintings show stormy seas crashing against the base of the castle rock.

It was considered that these were fanciful images, but studies of the first edition of the Ordnance Survey map of the area from 1860 show that the tide did reach the north end of the rock.

The Bamburgh Project has found evidence of an inlet which may have been used as a small port and it is possible that the sea would have run up against the rock along its east side in medieval times.

It was another storm in 1817 which blew away a mass of sand from the dunes to the south of the castle. This exposed human burials in cists, or stone-lined graves.

The Bamburgh Project has relocated this cemetery and each season of digging uncovers more burials.

The burials date from the 7th-8th Centuries and are thought to be of higher status individuals from the royal households of the Bamburgh kings. The individuals were strong and well fed. Buckles, brooches, knives and a silver pin have also been found.

Archaeologist Phil Wood says: "They seem to have always had good nutrition."

Bamburgh Castle is off the A1, on the B1341 or B1342.

Opening times are daily 11am-5pm, last entry 4.30pm, from March 12-October 31.

Admission is adult £5.50, concession £4.50, £2.50 for children from 6 to 15, under 6 it's free.

Tel: 01668 214 515.

The castle includes the Clock Tower tea rooms.

Alnwick Castle

Amongst the long list of illustrious names associated with Alnwick Castle over many centuries, we come to that of Harry Potter.

A castle of some description has been on the naturally defensive site of a bluff overlooking the River Aln for almost 900 years and has been the home of the Percy family – Earls and Dukes of Northumberland – for almost 700.

And what stories can be told from the history concentrated within and around the castle walls.

The magic of Potter has added a little more lustre to the castle and the current Duke is not complaining.

The inspirational castle and its setting has made it one of the most filmed locations in the North-East.

The films Harry Potter and the Philosopher's Stone and Harry Potter and the Chamber of Secrets took advantage of Alnwick.

That, and the opening of the Duchess of Northumberland's brainchild the Alnwick Garden has produced a surge in castle visitor numbers from 60,000 a year to up to 200,000.

"The gardens and Harry Potter have had a big effect," says the Duke.

Up to a third of Alnwick Garden visitors also take in the adjoining castle.

Other films partly shot at Alnwick include Becket with Peter O'Toole and

During the 17th Century Alnwick Castle slipped into decay and near dereliction.

When Charles I visited Alnwick it is recorded that the castle was "too ruinous to receive the king."

That changed when Elizabeth Seymour, a Percy descendant, arrived on the scene with her husband Hugh, Earl and then Duke of Northumberland.

She decided to turn the castle into their principal country seat and must have fully appreciated the task in hand when, on her first visit in 1751, the condition of the castle forced the couple to stay in the exchequer house.

The architects David Garrett, James Paine, and Robert Adam were all involved in the restoration works which included a suite of state rooms and a library.

Of the stone figures which line the upper reaches of the castle, those on the middle gateway and octagonal towers are medieval.

But those on other towers and the keep are from the 18th Century restoration when mason James Johnson of Stamfordham in Northumberland is believed to have devoted 20 years to carving the figures.

The great Northumbrian master gardener Capability Brown, who seems to have landscaped half of England, worked on the parkland surrounding the castle for the First Duke.

The 19th Century saw another wave of restoration.

Algernon, the Fourth Duke, commissioned the prolific County Durham architect Anthony Salvin, who built the Prudhoe Tower in honour of the Duke's creation as Baron Prudhoe.

Salvin added the present chapel, the Falconer's Tower and a guest hall.

A dinner was laid on for the workmen who had taken part in the restoration programme.

On each anniversary around 700 enjoyed roasts, pies, puddings, beer and pipes.

The Fourth Duke also engaged the Italian architect Luigi Canina, whom he had met in Rome in 1853 to mastermind the castle interiors.

A wood carving school was set up in Alnwick with 21 carvers and marble fireplaces were ordered from Italy.

The Italian influence is at its height in the castle saloon and drawing room. Hangings of Milanese silk, bought in 1864, still adorn their walls while 17th Century French tapestries acquired by the Duke decorate the chapel.

He was not the only dedicated collector to bring prized items to Alnwick. Elizabeth, the First Duchess, travelled in Europe in her own chaise followed by a coach full of servants and a wagon for her purchases.

But she would have been hard pressed to better the Fourth Duke who in Rome bought an entire gallery of important paintings in what has been described as the last and possibly biggest purchase at one go made by an Englishman abroad.

Richard Burton, Mary Queen of Scots with Vanessa Redgrave, Ivanhoe with Sam Neil, Robin Hood - Prince of Thieves with Kevin Costner, Elizabeth with Cate Blanchett and TV productions from the Antiques Roadshow and Treasure Hunt to the Clothes Show, Highway, Robin of Sherwood, Blackadder and even the Fast Show.

Such profile heightening is always welcome, especially when visitor revenue helps maintain this enormous defensive complex.

But Alnwick Castle is such a rich repository of so much heritage, architecture, history and art that is should need little in the way of assistance.

The beginnings of Alnwick Castle lie in the Norman age.

The site became the property of the Norman de Vescy family, whose barony provided the King with a dozen knights in time of need.

The Norman magnate Eustace built the stone castle which was described in 1138 as "most heavily fortified."

By its very nature and position, Alnwick Castle was regularly at the centre

Alnwick Castle and the lion bridge.

of conflict and history-making.

It passed into the hands of the Bishop of Durham, Antony Bec, who sold it in 1309 to Henry Percy and the essence of today's castle dates from the 14th Century.

In 1314 the garrison consisted of three knights, 38 armed soldiers and 40 hoblars, or mounted troopers.

It was not a lucky place for Scottish kings who came visiting with aggressive intentions.

In 1093 Malcolm Canmore, son of Duncan and victor over Macbeth, was killed just north of the castle across the River Aln.

In 1140 another Scottish king, William the Lion, was captured near the castle and imprisoned in Normandy.

Other Scots visitors include 6,000 prisoners taken at the Battle of Dunbar and who were lodged at the castle on their way to Durham.

Other lodgers fared better. In the Second World War pupils from Newcastle Church High School were evacuated to the castle.

Today, part of the castle accommodates American students from St Cloud State University in Minnesota.

No doubt the Americans delight in their venerable surroundings and may speculate on what life was like in the castle during its long existence.

A survey of 1538 shows that the castle's inhabitants were served by a bakehouse, brewhouse, military storehouse, cart sheds, stabling for 160 horses, and blackmith's shop.

A later inventory records that the inner bailey housed a garden, horse mill – vital in time of a siege – chantry and a school.

There were also two prisons, one in the gatehouse and the other a dungeon.

The Earls of Northumberland employed a considerable staff including steward of the household, purse bearer, foreign paymaster, clerk to the kitchen, gentleman of horse, gentleman usher, and disburser of apparel.

When the First Duchess of Northumberland arrived at Alnwick for the summer in 1768 her staff numbered 52, including 11 liveried footmen.

A perk for the laundry maids was a pitcher of ale on washdays.

The operation of the household changed after the restoration of the castle in the 19th Century, not least for the kitchen staff.

A hydraulic lift was installed capable of hoisting a ton of coal to fuel the roasting spit and ovens and to speed the delivery of food an

---

The Percy history is nothing if not dramatic.

The most famous of all the Percys, Harry Hotspur, battler against the Scots and the French and immortalised by Shakespeare, was born in the castle but died at the Battle of Shrewsbury in 1403.

Three Percy Earls were killed in battle, two were executed and two murdered.

Only two died in their beds.

The story starts with William de Percy, from the Caen area of France, who came to England as part of William the Conqueror's army.

The Alnwick-Percy link followed with:

Henry Percy (1273-1314) First Lord of Alnwick and regent in the king's absence.

Henry, (1314-1352) Second Lord of Alnwick, who in reward for his guardianship of the Border was given the barony of Warkworth and lordships of Rothbury and Newburn. He helped defeat the Scots at the Battle of Nevilles Cross in Durham in 1346.

Henry Percy (1368-1408), Marshal of England who was created Earl of Northumberland at the coronation of Richard II.

Henry, Second Earl (1403-1455) died fighting for the Lancastrian cause as did his son the Third Earl (1455-1461) at the Battle of Towton.

Henry, the Fourth Earl (1461-1489) was murdered by a mob of tenants incensed by the imposition of taxes.

The Fifth Earl (1489-1527) escorted Princess Margaret, daughter of Henry VII, north for her marriage to the Scottish king James IV.

Henry, the Sixth Earl (1527-1537) was caught up in the turmoil of Henry VIII's marriages and it fell to him to arrest Cardinal Wolsey.

Thomas, Seventh Earl (1557-1572) was executed for his part in the Rising of the North against Queen Elizabeth.

Henry, the Eighth Earl (1572-1585) was the victim of the official suspicion which now hung over his family and was imprisoned in the Tower of London, where he was found dead – probably murdered.

Henry, the Ninth Earl, was also held in the Tower for 17 years.

Algernon, the Tenth Earl (1632-1668) was Charles I's Lord High Admiral.

The Eleventh Earl (1668-1670) died on the Grand Tour.

Hugh, Earl and First Duke of Northumberland married Percy descendant Elizabeth Seymour, and they restored the castle and parkland.

Hugh, Second Duke (1786-1817) became a general in the American War of Independence. His Fifth Regiment of Foot became the Northumberland Fusiliers.

Hugh, Third Duke (1817-47) expanded the estates.

Algernon, Fourth Duke, (1847-65) restored the castle, served as a naval officer in the Napoleonic wars, and had a passion for travel and archaeological exploration.

The magnificent library at Alnwick Castle.

underground passage was built between the kitchen and the state dining room.

At the end of the 19th Century the household staff totalled 86, including six of each of laundry maids, housemaids, kitchen maids.

Of the family's other residences, Northumberland House in London was demolished for road development in 1874, Stanwick House in Yorkshire was sold in 1922 and Albury House in Surrey in 1965.

Syon House in London remains in the family.

The present Duke, while fully aware of the castle's great history, also has fond memories of it as a family home where he was born.

"The castle reflects a history of war and peace, cruelty and benevolence, of artistic patronage, building and innovation on a scale to rival any house in Britain," he says.

"I don't think we appreciated the works of art as we used our water pistols and kicked our footballs."

Because of the number of visitors, the family spend the summer in a house an hour's drive away from the castle.

Harry Potter, and history, see to that.

Alnwick Castle is easily reached off the A1. Alnwick Castle tea room, shop and grounds open at 10am and the castle at 11am, both until 5pm, daily from March 23 –October 28.

Admission: adult £7.95, concessions £7.50, children six-15 £2.95. Telephone 01665 510 777. 24-hour information line 01665 511 100.

Allen Gorge

While the North-East is blessed with often sublime scenery, there are some sights which are simply jaw-droppers.

Falling squarely into that category is Staward Gorge, which, with Allen Banks, makes up a stretch of blissfully beautiful river and woodland in Northumberland, and which is cared for by the National Trust.

Tucked just inside the North Pennines Area of Outstanding Natural Beauty, the estate of over 550 acres is made up of Allen Banks to the north,

including the "wilderness" walks linked to 19th Century Ridley Hall. In the middle of the estate is Plankey Mill, with its suspension bridge across the River Allen. To the south, is the rugged Staward Gorge. Visitors can walk from Allen Banks or Plankey Mill to the gorge, or from the opposite direction from Cupola Bridge. Either way, the view which opens up into

the jaws of the gorge from the path tucked into the crag high above the river, is stupendous.

The river threads its way through a ravine whose steep sides are cloaked in trees – a picture with more than a touch of grandeur. The gorge has impressed visitors for a long time. In 1761 the Rev Brown of nearby Whitfield wrote: "Upon the point of this high cliff you best may take your stand. It is indeed a prospect full of wonder."

On my visit the sense of being in a place apart was

© Barry Pells

Staward Gorge, part of the North Pennines Area of Outstanding Natural Beauty.

amplified by two buzzards soaring above, a heron flapping along the river and red squirrels racing up and down trees.

The North Pennines is characterised by open fells and heather moorland. Nevertheless, it is a surprise to learn that, with 43 trees per square kilometre, it has half as many trees as City of Westminster.

This means that Allen Banks and Staward Gorge, with its spectacular tree communities, is of especial importance.

Part of the woodland dates from medieval times and perhaps before, with

Although there are miles of footpaths around Allen Banks and Staward Gorge, there are three main walking circuits.

The Walks Wood along Raven Crag is a two-mile stroll which takes in the "wilderness" walks laid down by Susan Davidson of Ridley Hall, who also built several summerhouses en route. One of the summerhouses has been reconstructed using photographic evidence.

On the opposite side of the river is Morralee Wood and a walk of one-and-a-half miles including a tarn and the remains of old mineworkings and what is left of the Swiss Cottage summerhouse.

The bridge at Plankey Mill provides a circular walk from Allen Banks car park, taking in both banks of the river.

The walk from Plankey Mill in the middle of the estate to Staward Pele is two-and-a-half miles

with the option of continuing to Cupola Bridge. The walks are way-marked and colour-coded and they attract around 45,000 visitors a year.

A survey has shown that 56pc of visitors return at least once a month – a testimonial of satisfaction if ever there was one. The Allen Banks end of the estate is the most visited, with 90pc of arrivals using the car park and not venturing to Staward Gorge.

conifers and beech being planted in 1791. This has produced a mixture of native broadleaf trees such as ash, sessile oak, wych elm, birch, hazel, holly, bird cherry, alder, yew and rowan.

Between 1830 and 1860, Susan Davidson, who lived at Ridley Hall, enhanced Allen Banks with "wilderness" planting to contrast with the more formal planting and gardens around the property.

arry Pells

Cupola bridge over the River Allen.

Not surprisingly, the Allen Banks and Staward Gorge estate is as inviting for wildlife as it is for people.

Volunteers have made more than 20 visits and logged almost 70 different bird species.

They include common and honey buzzard, cuckoo, curlew, dipper, goosander, goshawk, great spotted woodpecker, kingfisher, peregrine, sand martin, spotted and pied flycatcher, tawny owl, tree creeper, willow and wood warbler and raven.

There are also red squirrel and otter. And the woods are particularly important for longhorn beetle, wet woodland cranefly and molluscs, and they accommodate seven out of the eight breeding species of bat found in the county.

In all, six species of creatures of national nature conservation concern breed in the woodlands in addition to six considered to be rare in Northumberland.

The area is also home to the only known colony of dormice in the region – the most northerly population in Britain.

Dormice nest-boxes have been installed and are being monitored.

After the death of her husband, she managed Ridley Hall estate and planned walks with stairs, bridges, an artificial pond, seats and summer-houses.

The quality and mix of the woodland guarantees an autumn colour extravaganza.

There are some bleak stands of conifers from when the Forestry Commission was manager in the '50s, before its multi-purpose forestry policy. Gloomy they may be, but they provide good conditions for fungi of which there is a bumper crop of every size and colour. It is one of the most important areas in the region for lichen.

A project to restore native woodland along the river is underway. Ancient woodland makes up only 1pc of Northumberland's area. Most of the sites are isolated with few over 150 acres, so the Allen Banks and Staward Gorge scheme is vital. Naturally-

People have left their mark on Allen Banks and the gorge over the centuries.

In the banks of the valley are coal seams and veins of lead ore and they have been worked for centuries. Lead was mined at Morralee Wood from 1856 to 1864 and again from 1881-82.

The remains of lime kilns can also be found in the area's woodlands. And high in an impregnable position above the gorge are the ruins of the fortification of Staward Pele.

The Romans first spotted its natural defensive advantages and the pele was built partially with Roman stone. An altar to Jupiter was also found on the site.

On three sides of the pele is a 200ft-drop. Only the narrow south-east neck of the site could be vulnerable but here a moat was dug and beyond is a field which was once probably marshland, with the only access via a narrow causeway.

The site may have been used in Anglo-Saxon times, with the word 'sta' meaning a fenced enclosure and 'ward' a yard.

King Edward II called for the building of a substantial pele tower to replace a timber blockhouse and palisade which occupied the site. Thomas de Featherstonehaugh, keeper of Tynedale, had built a tower on his home patch and no doubt felt qualified to take on the job. He offered to do it for £100 in four months, provided he could have all the necessary timber for free. Work started in 1326 but Thomas had under-estimated the task and in a letter to the king asked for more money and time.

In the same year the tower was completed, the king was deposed and died. It went to Edward III's wife Queen Philippa and in turn to one of her 11 children, Edmund Langley, who rented it to the canons of Hexham Priory.

A story linked to the ruins of Staward Pele suggests that Allen Banks is home to a multitude of wildlife.

the concept of 'The Sting' was alive and well centuries ago.

The tale concerns a man called Dicky the cattle thief, who made use of the ruins as a base. He stole two cattle from a farm near the Scottish border and drove them to Lanercost where he sold them to an unsuspecting farmer, who in turn allowed Dicky to stay the night. In the morning Dicky had vanished with the farmer's horse. On his way back to Staward Pele, he met the farmer whose beasts he had stolen and who asked Dicky if he had seen the missing cattle.

Dicky replied that he had – at Lanercost – and offered to sell the horse to the farmer so that he could make his way there quickly. The sale was completed but the comments of the two farmers, when the penny dropped, have unfortunately not been passed down to us.

developing broad leaf woodland with a large proportion of dead trees – important to wild-life – are in short supply.

It's another reason to nurture the Allen stretch – the most extensive area of ancient woodland in Northumberland. Conifer stands are being thinned and coppicing is taking place, along with natural regeneration of native trees and new planting in what is a £100,000 project which began in 1998.

Trust property manager and woodland project officer Denis Fleming says: "As well as the gorge and its ridge above the river with shingle banks, there's a traditional agricultural landscape and meadows, footpaths and tranquillity. There is no other gorge in Northumberland of this grandeur. It's magnificent. Nowhere compares with it and there is nothing as dramatic as that gorge view."

Francis Bowes-Lyon, who inherited the property and gave it to the trust in 1942, would have agreed. He wrote: "I've given my property to the National Trust in the hope this lovely stretch of woodland and river scenery may continue to give others the immense enjoyment that it has given my family and myself for many years."

Allen Banks car park is between Haydon Bridge and Bardon Mill and is signposted off the A69.

The car park has a leaflet dispenser and picnic site. It is open all year and costs £1 for half a day and £2 for a full day. Tel: (01434) 344-218.

Plankey Mill is reached via a signed minor road off the A686 just past Langley Castle.

Cupola Bridge is further along the A686, before the Whitfield turn-off.

The setting of Housesteads, straddled on top of the towering Whin Sill crags overlooking what is still today a sweeping, open vista with a touch of wilderness, is one of the reasons why it is probably the most popular attraction on Hadrian's Wall.

Looking from the top of the ridge towards Wark Forest, it is easy to feel that this was indeed the northern edge of the Roman Empire. It was certainly at the fringe of civilized society during the centuries of Anglo-Scottish conflict as the province of thieves and brigands until the end of the 16th Century. Such was the area's reputation that the Elizabethan antiquaries Camden and Cotton were afraid to visit because of "the rank robbers thereabouts". Even up to the last years of the 17th

Housesteads

Thousand of walkers have tackled the Hadrian's Wall national trail. But few will know that they are following in the footsteps of William Hutton, a Quaker who at the age of 78 trekked the length of the wall in 1801. The highlight of his adventure, it seems, was Housesteads fort in Northumberland, which he described as "the greatest station on the whole line. Here lies the ancient splendour in bold characters".

Above: Mithras Temple, Hadrian's Wall.

Century, the land was owned by a notorious, horse-rustling branch of the Armstrong clan.

When the antiquarian William Stuckley visited in 1725, it was still not easy going as the Military Road which follows the line of the wall had yet to be built. But Stuckley was still mightily impressed with Housesteads. He wrote that the remains looked "as ruined but yesterday" and produced a drawing showing a landscape scattered with altars, sculptures and carved stones.

Today, after 150 years of excavation, Housesteads is the most complete, and best preserved, example of a Roman fort in Britain. If the five-acre fort makes a major impact on its 120,000 annual visitors, we can image the effect, when it was built, on the local population, for whom 'big' was a cluster of roundhouses. That could

For James Crow, one of the factors which makes Housesteads special is that it was one of the first forts in the Roman Empire to be fully excavated at the end of the 19th Century.

James has himself conducted major excavations on Hadrian's Wall and has written a book on Housesteads.

Digging began in 1822 supervised by Rev John Hodgson.

Then came John Clayton, town clerk of Newcastle, whose family owned nearby Chesters. To preserve as much of the wall as possible, he bought up land – Housesteads included – where he continued the excavations.

James says: "Housesteads has a reputation it deserves for the most extensive remains on Hadrian's Wall and in what is the finest setting.

"There is the great sweep of the Whin Sill to the east, spectacular views south, forests to the north, and the feeling of isolation.

"People appreciate all the activity which was at Housesteads, the buildings and the sophistication in what was a very wild place by anybody's standards.

"It evokes Rome, but it couldn't be more distant from Rome. It is that unique combination which gives Housesteads the edge."

He says its appeal is the sense of loss of what has been. "But given that so many people lived there because the Romans were there, when the Romans left there was no reason to sit on the top of that hill."

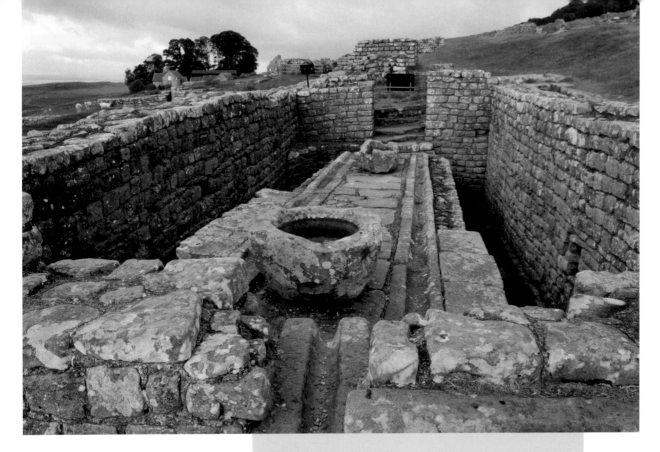

have led to what was likely to have been the original name of Vercovicium for the fort, which was found on an altar to the god Mars.

According to James Crow, senior lecturer in Roman archaeology at Newcastle University, native names were often adopted for forts. On this basis, Vercovicium would translate as the "place of the effective fighters", which may have been applied by locals to the first Roman garrison.

The original fort had at least 10 barracks for what was an infantry force. The soldiers were served by a hospital and a bath house outside

Tucked away in a corner of Housesteads is the fort's main attraction, the latrines.

Excavation has shown that there was a continuous row of lavatory seats above a deep sewer flowing in an anti-clockwise direction. There was no privacy.

The facility was sited at this low corner of the fort so that surface and drainage water could be channeled to clean the sewer. The flushing system was only effective during or after rain and an open sandstone cistern holding up to 2,800 gallons was built to collect water from a nearby tower roof. A water channel also ran around the central platform of the latrines. This was thought to have been used to clean sponges but some experts now doubt that sufficient of the Mediterranean sea creatures could have been imported to satisfy the needs of the Roman army in Britain.

the base close to the Knag Burn which flows through the Whin Sill escarpment. Baths were later built inside the fort, perhaps because the first site had become too exposed and dangerous. The commander's house was constructed to a

courtyard plan familiar across the Roman Empire but a design meant to provide shade from the Mediterranean sun was adapted at Housesteads to give protection from the prevailing winds. The house had a dining room with underfloor heating and heated flues in the walls.

There were four gates at the fort. A sculpture of Victory which adorned the East Gate has survived. Here deeply-worn wheel ruts are preserved at 4ft 8ins apart - the normal width of cart axles - which is also reflected in the standard rail gauge.

There were granaries, a bakehouse, and the headquarters complex. The sculpture of Mars which was placed over the entrance to the headquarters building is another survivor. The basic plan of the barracks remained the same for almost 200 years. But there were big changes at the end of the Third Century at the same time as the fort's defences were subject to major rebuilding. Instead of having one long roof running the full length of the barracks, each of the new barracks had its own roof rather like a series of chalets with a narrow alley between each. They had different features based on the choices of the occupants. One theory is that instead of barracks occupied by troops, the chalets were family houses.

With the breakdown of Roman control, what for centuries had been a thriving, populous centre of fort and nearby civilian settlement dwindled to the handful of people who have lived in the area since then.

James Crow says: "Since the end of Roman rule, the population at Housesteads is unlikely to have ever exceeded 20 to 30 persons.

"Once Imperial authority and payments were severed, the garrison and their dependants left, rather like an old mining town after the goldrush."

What they left behind, and the sense of emptiness which returned, is the magnet which draws the crowds back today.

The garrison at Housesteads, recorded on inscriptions from the site, were the First Cohort of Tungrians.

The Roman army was divided into legions – regular troops who built the wall and were stationed at large bases like York and Chesters – and auxiliaries. It was auxiliaries, recruited from lands subdued by the Romans, who garrisoned Hadrian's Wall.

The Tungrians were from a Germanic tribe living in what is now southern Belgium and Holland. In the early Third Century Housesteads garrison was boosted by units of Frisian troops, from eastern Holland and Germany and another group of Germans named on an altar in words which translate as "Notfried's Own" – probably the man who raised the troop.

Where there were hundreds of soldiers with pay, there were camp followers, traders and merchants all living in the civilian settlement, or vicus, below the fort.

When one of the houses was excavated, the remains of two skeletons were found sealed under a layer of clay.

One was of a tall man and within his ribs was the point of a knife. The other skeleton is thought to have been that of a woman. There seems no doubt that the couple had been murdered and the crime successfully hidden for 1,700 years.

Housesteads is owned by the National Trust and managed by English Heritage.

It is off the B6318. Telephone (01434) 344363. It is open from October 1-March 31 10am-4pm daily and from March 24 - September 30 from 10am-6pm.

Admission: adults £3.60, concessions £2.70, children £1.80, family ticket £9.

Crag Lough sits under the towering cliff face of the Whin Sill.

Hadrian's Wall Loughs

Beauty runs deep in Northumberland's lake land, which is found along the central section of Hadrian's Wall.

The vistas are hugely impressive along the six-mile, 2,820-acre estate mostly owned by the National Trust and which lies in Northumberland National Park. While the wall itself is the prime feature of what is a world heritage site, the grandeur of the surrounding scenery provides the perfect setting. And a major feature in this landscape are what are known as the Roman Wall loughs, or lakes. The North-East, unlike neighbouring Cumbria, is not known for its natural lakes. For this reason alone the shallow, Greenlee, Broomlee, Crag and Grindon loughs are special places.

They were created by Ice Age glacial action which scooped out the soft shale to leave cavities that filled with water.

Crag Lough, beneath the sheer face of the Whin Sill ridge, is one of the definitive views of Hadrian's Wall country.

The earliest evidence of human activity in the area comes from a study by Newcastle University of ancient botanical and environmental evidence in deposits in Crag Lough.

The study showed a decline in trees and an increase in grass pollens and plants such as corn buttercup, typical of open

The importance of Greenlee Lough is such that it has been designated a national nature reserve. It has some of Britain's rarest habitats which have declined over the last century. Covering 18 acres, it is the biggest natural lake in Northumberland. Various plans to turn Greenlee Lough into a fish farm then a chalet complex with power boats on the lough led to Northumberland National Park buying the site 14 years ago. The adjoining Greenlee Farm is also owned by the park and the tenancy agreement includes provision for access to the reserve.

The park has provided a bird hide and a one-mile way-marked trail around the reserve,

with boardwalks over the fragile mire and fen habitats. Park voluntary wardens laid the boardwalk's 2,285 planks of redwood in just four days.

Neighbouring land at Stonefolds was bought by the park in 1999 with the backing of the Heritage Lottery Fund. The lough is home to pike and perch. In the past, pike caught on nightlines were fed to the sheepdogs at Greenlee Farm.

The water is also used by whooper and mute swans, goldeneye, tufted duck, goosander, teal, coot and widgeon.

The insect population of the lough includes four species of dragonfly and damselfly, 70 species of moth and 30 of spiders.

The fact that there are few artificial nutrients favours various water vegetation. Around the lough are plants such as marsh cinquefoil and its crimson flowers and strawberry-like fruit, skullcap, flag iris, water mint, angelica, sneezewort, and ragged robin.

The lough's reedbeds, at 790ft above sea level, are a rare habitat and shelter reed buntings and sedge warblers.

Around the edges of the lough are peat deposits many feet thick, which have formed domes. These raised bogs have grown over thousands of years. In the past they have been damaged by drainage. But now the water table is being raised by more than 200 plywood dams

which block old drainage channels.

Although now quiet, Greenlee Lough has been used in the past. Nearby Bonnyrigg Hall was a country residence and shooting and fishing sporting estate of the Blackett family,

Deep in the reed bed and marshy woodland are the roofless remnants of a Victorian boat house.

Park ecologist Gillian Thompson says: "The Roman Wall loughs are of international importance. Natural water bodies are very infrequent in the North-East.

"People tend to stay immediately around Hadrian's Wall and very few get out to places like Greenlee Lough. It's an unspoilt jewel."

The Sycamore Gap, as featured in the 1991 Kevin Costner film, Prince of Thieves, set around the Robin Hood legend.

fields, trackways and areas of deliberate clearance. Although tree cover was reduced, hazel was kept for coppicing for stakes and for its nuts.

The loughs are part of a site of special scientific interest and a European Special Area of Conservation. They are all that remains of a bigger collection of lakes which were still to be seen in the 18th Century but which were then drained. Another of the loughs, Little Caw, has since silted up and filled with vegetation. This is what is likely to happen to the surviving loughs over the coming centuries.

Broomlee and Greenlee, just to the north of Housesteads fort on the wall, are only around 6ft to 8ft deep. What is striking is that while the wall, especially the three-mile stretch from Housesteads west to Steel Rigg, is busy with walkers and the fort itself is a honeypot for visitors, a short distance to the north there is an air of remoteness around the loughs.

Crag and Broomlee loughs are owned by the National Trust and Greenlee Lough by Northumberland National Park.

The Pennine Way runs through a gap in the Whin Sill crags and takes walkers close to Broomlee and Greenlee.

It is then possible to experience a view which few people do - that of seeing the crags and the wall by looking south.

"Just a short walk to the north of the wall and there is this feeling of total remoteness even now," says Andrew Poad, National Trust property manager for the Hadrian's Wall estate.

"Crag Lough, sitting under its crags, is one of the iconic views of Hadrian's Wall and gives you the sense of being right on the edge of something."

Paget Lazarri, national park senior ranger, says of the loughs area: "Very few people actually walk north and look back for what is a very dramatic view of crags which are a real obstacle, and the wall running along the top.

"You can imagine looking at that view 2,000 years ago. It would have had a real impact and you would have felt that you didn't want to mess with the people on the other side of the wall.

"There is still a sense of isolation out there."

As well as the Pennine Way route, visitors can take a three-mile circular walk from Steel Rigg car park to skirt Crag Lough and Hotbank which also gives views south to the Whin Sill and the wall.

Andrew's favourite view is from Sewingshields Crags just east of Housesteads, looking down on to Broomlee Lough. Sewingshields is the last major outcrop to the east on Hadrian's Wall of the Whin Sill which, from the Tipalt Burn on the Cumbria border, often presents a craggy face to the north, peaking at a height of more than 1,000ft at Whinshields Crags.

"Looking down on Broomlee Lough from Sewingshields Crags is a fantastic view and you probably won't see a soul," says Andrew.

"If you head off on the Pennine Way, you leave heavily-used areas but once you are over the hill top you are in the middle of nowhere in a wilderness which is fabulous."

There is a legend of buried treasure in Broomlee Lough - perhaps linked to prehistoric practices of making votive offerings in watery places. But attempts by divers to locate any hoard were unsuccessful.

The lough has healthy populations of the nationally-declining native crayfish, and otters. The loughs and the crags are places of curlews and crows. The Whin Sill, formed by quartz dolerite whinstone 295 million years ago, offers walks along one of the classic stretches of wall country.

Heading west from Housesteads there are the views along Cuddy's Crags, Hotbank Crags and Peel Crags.

"In terms of views, I think the central section of the wall is rivaled only by the Northumbrian coast," says Andrew.

The Whin Sill is punctuated by gaps, or nicks, caused by the overflow channels of ice-dammed lakes around 12,000 years ago.

Busy Gap near Sewingshields Crags was described in the 16th Century as being a 'common entry of all thieves'.

The ravine of Milky Gap is named after the milking cattle which grazed the rough pasture north of the wall.

There are Castle Nick and Peel gaps, and Rapinshaw Gap where the Pennine Way threads through the wall.

Then there is Sycamore Gap. This is a relatively recent name which comes from the solitary tree

© NTPL

Hadrian's Wall

growing in the break in the crags. It was part of John Clayton's 19th Century estate, and Andrew says: "The Victorians had an eye for landscapes and it wouldn't surprise me if the tree had not been planted deliberately at that time."

It featured in the 1991 Kevin Costner film Prince of Thieves, based on the Robin Hood legend. In one scene a boy takes refuge in the tree.

"Years after the film, people still stop and take photographs of the tree and parents put their children in the tree and take pictures," says Andrew.

"It is slightly alarming that Hollywood can write its own history."

Just east of Sewingshields Crags are two of the most interesting religious sites to have been found from Roman Britain. Near the fort of Carrawburgh was the shrine and temple of Coventina, thought to be a local goddess. It included a well in which was found 15,000 Roman coins which had been deposited as offerings, along with jewellery and the model of a terrier dog.

Nearby is the Mithraeum, which had been buried for more than 1,600 years before being discovered in 1949. This was a temple to the god Mithras and was probably built by the garrison of the fort. Three altars – dedicated by commanding officers – were found, copies of which stand in the temple remains. Mithras was an Eastern god. According to the legend, Mithras killed the primeval bull – the first creature created on Earth – in a cave. Temples to the god were deliberately gloomy in order to resemble a cave. On one altar Mithras appears as the Charioteer of the Sun. The stone was hollowed out so that a lamp placed behind would light up the sun's rays. Above the altar would have been a sculpture of Mithras killing the bull. The original altars and sculptures are in the Museum of Antiquities at Newcastle University.

The site is managed by English Heritage and there is a car park off the B6318 four miles west of Chollerford.

North Pennines

When it comes to a natural beauty contest, the North Pennines has some pretty tough competition. It lies between the national parks of Northumberland, the Lake District and the Yorkshire Dales.

But the North Pennines can more than hold its own. At almost 2,000 square kilometres, it is the second biggest of the country's 41 Areas of Outstanding Natural Beauty and is larger than all but two of the family of national parks.

A third of the North Pennines AONB is made up of sites of special scientific interest. There are two national nature reserves, including Britain's biggest at Moor House-Upper Teesdale and five European Special Areas of Conservation. Only 20pc of the landscape has been significantly agriculturally improved and a mere 0.6pc is considered as built up.

It could be argued that the North-East as a whole has a greater stake in the North Pennines than any other part of the region. The three great rivers which characterise the region, the Tyne, Wear and Tees, all rise in the North Pennines.

The AONB straddles Northumberland, County Durham and Cumbria and lies within the boundaries of Carlisle, Eden, Derwentside, Teesdale, Tynedale and Wear Valley.

The very rocks which underpin the North Pennines and frame its landscape are of such international importance that the area was designated as Britain's first European geo-park. The North Pennines is taking a leading role among 17 European Geo-parks in helping UNESCO to establish a worldwide network.

The rocks of the North Pennines tell the stories of mountain building and erosion, ice flows and tropical seas, minerals and miners. The tourism potential is hinted at by the fact that the area now holds an annual Northern Rocks festival in May and June.

Geologists have tracked the story of the North Pennines back to almost 500 million years ago, from when the oldest rocks date. Then, what was to be the North Pennines lay south of the equator, where it formed part of the deep Lapetus Ocean on the edge of a continent called Eastern Avalonia. This collided with another continent, Laurentia, which destroyed the ocean and the crumpling of rocks produced a mountain chain across what is northern England.

By 360 million years ago the area had moved to a position astride the equator and much of what is now northern England was submerged underneath a tropical sea where beds of limestone accumulated. Sand and mud developed into land with tropical forests, producing coal, sandstone and mudstone.

Around 295 million years ago molten rock spread out as sheets between existing rock and formed the dolerite of the Whin Sill, the dramatic feature which runs across much of the north and is seen at Hadrian's Wall, in Teesdale at High Force and Cauldron Snout, and High Cup Nick.

Mineral-rich waters seeped through cracks and faults in the rocks, forming crystallised mineral deposits.

By 280 million years ago, what was to be the North Pennines became an arid desert, leaving behind the red and pink Penrith sandstone. Around two million years ago the ice cover and melting helped shape today's landscape.

Dark limestone known as Frosterley marble, which contains prominent marine fossils, has been worked since the 14th Century and was used in Durham Cathedral. It also appears in York Minster, Norwich RC Cathedral, and Truro and Bombay cathedrals.

One dramatic 300-million-year-old relic is a large fossilised tree stump and roots which was extracted from a quarry in Edmundbyers and is on show in Stanhope churchyard.

Several minerals were first discovered in the North Pennines including witherite on Alston Moor by Dr William Witherite in 1783, Alstonite in 1835 and Brianyoungite, which was found by Northumberland geologist Brian Young in 1993. A geodiversity action plan for the area puts forward more than 60 sites as places with visitor potential.

Geological tourism could be the next big thing for the North Pennines, feels AONB officer Chris Woodley-Stewart.

Chris works for the North Pennines AONB Partnership, which is made up of almost 30 bodies. He is particularly enthusiastic about the leading role being played by the North Pennines in the emerging international network of geo-parks. "It is a feather in our caps. In 10 years' time everybody will know what a geo-park is," he predicts.

"There are a lot of places in the North Pennines which could be used for geological tourism. The area was one of the birthplaces of geological science."

What makes the North Pennines special for Chris is "the sense of wilderness and remoteness, the high moors, the blanket bogs, the wading birds, hay meadows, geology, the rich history. Put all that together and you have the North Pennines."

A management plan has just been produced to conserve and enhance the area's natural beauty.

"That beauty will be a driving force in the future economy of the North Pennines," he says.

It also happens to be one of the most remote and unspoilt places left in England, and this increasingly rare commodity is central to its appeal. After all, there are few spots in England where you can walk all day and not cross a road.

In 1842, investigating conditions in the lead mines, W R Mitchell was giving evidence to the Royal Commission into Children's Employment.

He wrote of the North Pennines: "From it flows the Tyne, the Wear and the Tees and many branches of these rivers.

"Along the banks are dales or valleys, cultivated near the banks and for a short distance up the sides of the fells. But soon cultivation and enclosure cease, and beyond them the dark fells covered with peat and moss and heath, and between one vale and another is a wide extend of high moorland."

Not much has changed. If anything, as the rest of the country has become increasingly developed and congested, the sense of space in the North Pennines has widened. Today, the North Pennines has a population of around 12,000 - less than half of what it was in 1861.

In the 18th Century,

Old packhorse routes across the North Pennines are being used as walking trails. The most direct route for the lead from the North Pennines to the Tyne for shipping to the rest of Britain and abroad was across the fells and moors and for many years it was the Galloway packhorse in strings of 15 to 20 animals which provided the means of transport.

Durham County Council has produced a pack of three walks based on the routes and another two general lead mining heritage rambles. There are plans to improve public access to the area by developing nine packhorse trails for riders, walkers and cyclists. Some of the place names in the North Pennines provide clues to the packhorse past. Jingling Gate near Lord's Lot in Hexhamshire probably refers to bells attached to the lead horse and which would have jingled when the animal passed through the gateway. There is also Carriers Hill near Killhope and Galloway Hill near Causeway Top between Weardale and Teesdale.

travellers did not like what they perceived as the wild and threatening moorland.

Now the landscape is highly valued and sustainable tourism is seen as a major economic provider.

The North Pennines inspires visitors just as it did the poet W H Auden. Many of his poems in the 1920-30s and two of his plays are set in the area.

The open moorland and high grasslands are not exactly empty. They accommodate 22,000 pairs of breeding birds.

In some areas there are more than 90 pairs per square kilometre – one of the highest breeding densities in Britain.

The area is home to 12pc of Britain's merlin population, 10pc of its golden plover, and 80pc of England's black grouse. Songbirds like skylark, meadow pipit and ring ouzel which are in decline elsewhere are abundant in the North Pennines. The dales support 40pc of the UK's upland hay meadows, which are important to yellow wagtail, redshank, and lapwing.

The highest land in England outside the Lake District is found in the North Pennines. And if you like extremes, then the average summer temperature at Cow Green is the same as that in Reykjavik in Iceland.

High House Chapel, Ireshopeburn.

Volunteers rally round to run the Weardale Museum based in what was once a Methodist minister's manse in Ireshopeburn. Next door is the High House Chapel. It is the oldest Methodist chapel in the world in continuous weekly use since its foundation in 1760. John Wesley's many visits to Weardale, the history of the chapel and the growth of Methodism, are chronicled in the museum. It contains a dedicated Wesley Room with many examples of Methodist memorabilia.

There is also a Weardale kitchen furnished as it would have been for lead-mining and farming families 100 years ago. The museum tells the stories of the Westgate Subscription Library, established in 1788 by the early Methodist Society, the history of railways in Weardale, and has the complete census records for Stanhope Parish 1841-1901 as well as a superb collection of local crystallised minerals and fossils.

The museum is open from 2pm-5pm May to September (except Monday and Tuesday)

It is open every afternoon in August and Easter and Bank Holidays and for groups at any time by appointment.

For further information telephone: (01388) 537417 or (01388) 517433.

Left: Howick Hall built by 18th Century architect William Newton.

Right: The vibrant Howick Hall Gardens.

Howick

Earl Grey, looking down from his column in the centre of Newcastle, would no doubt approve of the monumental undertakings at his ancestral home of Howick Hall in Northumberland. The present Lord Howick of Glendale is carrying on the family tradition of planting by building up an enviable arboretum - or collection of exotic trees and shrubs. Since 1985, he has sallied forth on expeditions across the world to bring back seed from the wild to grow on at the nursery at Howick Hall, just south of Craster, for the arboretum which is being developed in meadowland.

His trips, sanctioned by permits and carried out on a scientific basis, have seen him visit China 10 times, North America three times, Japan twice, and also India, the Himalayas, New Zealand and Europe. The result so far is a collection of 10,500 specimens in the arboretum, spanning 1,700 different varieties.

"It's probably one of the largest wild collected arboretums in the country.

"It is all properly documented and so it is of

Lord Howick relaxing in the tranquil setting of Howick Gardens.

Howick has been the home of the Grey family since 1319. The hall was built by 18th Century Newcastle architect William Newton for the bachelor Sir Henry Grey. On his death, it passed to the 2nd Earl Grey, who had 16 children.

The main body of the hall has been empty since 1967. The present Lord Howick, and wife Clare live in the west wing. They have three grown-up daughters, Rachel, Jessica and Alice, and a son, David.

"The hall was getting very expensive and my mother just got fed up," says Lord Howick.

The main reception rooms are on the ground floor, with nine bedrooms on the first floor, and another seven on the top floor.

"It would cost an arm and a leg to run the place. If I had written the Harry Potter stories then I would be living in it," says Lord Howick.

"But there is a lot of curiosity about the hall."

There are plans to open up the ground floor to house a botanical exhibition and a display telling the history of the family.

to do with the fact that the attraction has not exactly been aggressively marketed. That's the way Lord Howick wants it.

Two years ago, there were 8,000 visitors, many of them regulars and others coming by word of mouth. Last year that figure rose to 11,500 as a spin-off from the opening of nearby Alnwick Castle gardens.

"Many of the gardens which are open to the public and which are not commercialised and concentrate on being as natural as possible are getting fewer and fewer," says Lord Howick.

"We want to retain that natural quality here. The emphasis is on a pleasant informality where people can come to get away from the kitchen and the kids.

use to botanists," says Lord Howick. Yet the arboretum is just one of the surprise delights of Howick Hall and its gardens.

The gardens, run by a charitable trust chaired by Lord Howick, are open to the public. The sense of tranquillity and the relaxed passage of time has much

As well as his achievements as a leading 19th Century politician, the 2nd Earl Grey's other claim to fame is the bergamot-flavoured tea which is named after him. So it seemed entirely logical that the Earl Grey tea rooms were opened at Howick Hall. And more stately tea rooms you would be hard pressed to find.

They are housed in what was originally the conservatory and which in the 1850s became a ballroom and then served as a convalescent hospital for soldiers in the two world wars. The rooms, with their wood panels and oil paintings, offer a dozen types of tea.

The business is run by Rosie Robson, who lives at the Old Rectory, Howick, and whose husband Neil has the celebrated Robsons kipper-smoking business in the nearby coastal village of Craster. Rosie uses Craster kippers and salmon, and other local produce.

There are touches such as the use for afternoon tea of etageres,

the three-tier stands which carry finger sandwiches, fresh scones and jam and cream. Herbal infusions are served in glass pots so that the process can be observed.

Rosie has had links with the Howick estate for more than 20 years.

She says: "We wanted to stick to something which was traditionally English. I thought tea rooms would complement the gardens if it was done in the right way.

"I wanted it to be part of the history and beauty of the place. The whole place has a very peaceful ambience and I have tried to continue this in the tea rooms.

"I have been all over the world but Howick and its gardens are a little bit of heaven.

"It is a very special, unspoilt place and there aren't many like it left today."

Famous for his bergamot-flavoured tea, the 2nd Earl Grey at Howick.

"The gardens are deliberately aimed at garden lovers and we intend to keep them free from commercial exploitation.

"There may be a few surplus plants for sale and perhaps the odd postcard, but that's it," said Lord Howick, who is also a trustee of the botanic garden at Edinburgh.

For the discerning visitor, the stance against

commercialisation pays dividends. The woodland garden harbours islands of colour from rhododendrons, azaleas, magnolias, camellias, primula and the meconopsis blue poppy. Being just over a mile from the sea offers protection against severe frost and enables tender specimens to do well.

The woodland garden was started in the 1930s by Lord Howick's grandfather, the 5th Earl Grey. Both he and his wife were enthusiastic

gardeners. In fact Howick, with tens of thousands of daffodils in various varieties, has one of the best displays of the flower in the UK.

Leaving the woodland garden with its heady scents, the next treat is the meadow grassland studded with tulips – an effect created by Lord Howick's mother, Lady Mary.

"She called it her Botticelli meadow," says Lord Howick.

Above: Rosie Robson in the Howick Hall tea rooms.

Right: Howick Hall Church.

An on-going project is the shaping of a bog garden around a pond, featuring herbaceous plants grown from wild seed. The pond has been fashioned from a naturally swampy area. "It has always been a bit of a sump," says Lord Howick.

When the adjacent Howick Hall was constructed in 1782, the builders were sufficiently concerned to dig a deep trench to drain away the water in the area.

Having taken a turn around the gardens, the Long Walk beckons visitors. This stretches for one and a half miles from the woodland garden, following the wooded dene of the Howick Burn to the sea. A short way into the walk, off to the side, is what was once a fishing lake and now a haven for water lilies, and nesting swans, herons, ducks and water hen.

The dene was re-planted with beech by the 2nd Earl Grey, who, as Prime Minister, was responsible for the passage of the Great Reform Bill of 1832 – hence the Newcastle column and statue. His marble tomb is in the chapel within the gardens.

Among the old gravestones surrounding the chapel is the last resting place of five French sailors, whose bodies were found on the shore after their vessel sank in 1911.

The 2nd Earl's tomb once had a Gothic marble canopy but this was demolished by the 5th Earl, using a hammer and chisel.

"He hated it. If that sort of thing happened today it would give English Heritage a heart attack," says Lord Howick.

As it is, it just happens to be one of the many curiosities hidden away at Howick.

Howick Hall is six miles north east of Alnwick of the B1339 on the coast between Boulmer and Craster.

The gardens are open daily from 1pm-6pm until late October.

Admission is £3 adults, £2 pensioners. Children free. No dogs.

Telephone 01665 577 285.

Raby Castle

When it comes to the castles capital of Britain, Northumberland has to be a leading contender.

But neighbouring County Durham was not immune from the troubles which encouraged the building of castles in the first place. County Durham certainly has its share - and Raby Castle leads the way.

The powerful Nevill family built the 14th Century castle which forms the basis of what can be seen today.

It was in the castle's Baron's Hall that 700 notables gathered to plot the Rising of the North, the failure of which forced Sir Charles Nevill to flee to Holland in 1569 with his lands forfeit to the Crown.

In 1626, Sir Henry Vane, later treasurer to Charles I, bought Raby and his descendants still own the place with the 11th Lord Barnard the current incumbent.

But Raby is more than a castle. There are five acres of gardens, a deer park, and coach house with a collection of carriages that includes the Raby State Coach, last used in 1902 for the Coronation of Edward VII.

Visitors enter the castle through the 62ft high Nevill Gateway, equipped with conduits from which boiling water or oil, or other unsavoury concoctions, could be poured on attackers. This was a castle which was difficult to crack, given that the width of the walls of the 79ft high Cliffords Tower are 9ft thick, even at the top. Another four towers adorn the castle.

At one end of the scale, a highlight of Raby Castle is the richly decorated Octagon Drawing Room, dating from the 1840s and awash with sumptuous textiles and gilding. Gold silk lines the eight walls and the curtains are of crimson and gold silk. In 1993 a programme of restoration began which included the renovation of textiles described by the Victoria and Albert Museum in London as astonishing in quality and quantity. Where it was impossible to conserve silks, new material was woven on the only 19th Century hand looms still is use in England.

The suite of gilded furniture supplied by a Bond Street, London, company had been dispersed throughout the castle but, using an 1864 inventory, this was reassembled and covered in red and gold silks to match the curtains, as was the case 150 years ago.

By contrast, another highlight is the kitchen, which almost completely retains its medieval form. Today householders keeping pace with changing kitchen fashions have fuelled a substantial industry. At Raby, the kitchen was in use for 600 years until 1954. A ceiling vault with four intersecting arches sweeps upwards to a ventilation shaft, providing an updraught to remove smoke and fumes. Across the corners of the kitchen are massive beams, from which sides of meat and hams were hung by ropes fastened to pegs which can still be seen. Around the kitchen runs a passageway set within the thick walls. It doubled as a serving passageway to the Baron's Hall and as a defensive emplacement manned by soldiers.

The castle's entrance hall, part of the original medieval structure, was created in its present form in the 18th Century to allow carriages to be driven through to the hall itself. The 10th Lord and Lady Barnard would have their horses brought into the hall before riding off to join the Hunt.

The hall is decorated with a circle of Brown Bess muskets and bayonets, which were used by the South Durham Militia, as well as Cromwell helmets and the sword used by the 2nd Earl at the Battle of Fontenoy.

On a more everyday note, there is a leather-covered porter's chair with sides to shield the occupant from

A short drive from Raby Castle is the ancestral home of a North-East figure made famous by the song – Bonnie Bobby Shafto.

The listed Whitworth Hall near Spennymoor was home to the Shafto family for more than 300 years and sits at the heart of a 73-acre deer park. The hall is now a 29-bedroom hotel.

There is free entry to the country park, where feeding the deer is a popular family activity. Visitors can also enjoy the hall's walled gardens, and the most northerly vineyard in England, plus fishing in an ornamental lake and the Shafto Inn and restaurant.

Bonnie Bobby Shafto held the estate for 55 years from 1742. In 1774 Bobby married Anne Duncombe, of Duncombe Park, Helmsley in Yorkshire. He was elected MP for Durham City at the age of 30.

More verses were added to the song when his grandson, Robert Duncombe Shafto, campaigned successfully in the 1861 election for the Durham seat. Bobby died in 1797 and is buried in the Shafto crypt at Whitworth Church near the hall.

draughts and a cupboard below which held a pot of glowing charcoal.

After the grand rooms comes the Servants' Hall which is also thought to have been the guardroom.

Lunch was the only meal eaten in the hall by all the servants, and had a hierarchy and ritual all of its own. After the first course the butler, housekeeper, and lady's maid would retire to the housekeeper's room to finish the meal. The cook never joined the other servants but was served in the cook's sitting room next to the kitchen.

The large jugs in the Servants' Hall once contained beer which accompanied lunch and there are also the mahogany wheeled trays which were pushed up and down the table to supply bread.

Raby attracts almost 30,000 visitors a year and castle spokeswoman Catherine Turnbull says: "It is as equally good as Northumberland castles if indeed it does not exceed them. It is imposing both inside and outside.

"It has a stately home feel but it is not a museum. It is lived in and is a warm and welcoming place to visit."

The first mention of Raby, then spelt Rabi, was in the reign of King Cnut in the 11th Century.

In the 14th Century, the owner of Raby, Ralph Nevill, took Scottish King David II prisoner at the Battle of Nevill's Cross. He was a great benefactor of the church and was the first layman to be buried in Durham Cathedral.

A succeeding Ralph Nevill is mentioned by Shakespeare in Henry V and as created Earl of Westmorland.

The father of 21 children, he was Earl Marshall of England and his youngest daughter Cicely was the mother of Edward IV and Richard III.

Raby Castle is near Staindrop in County Durham and is off the A688.

Opening times are daily except Saturdays in June, July and August. May and September Wednesday and Sunday only.

The castle is open from 1pm-5pm and the gardens from 11am-5.30pm

Admission is castle, park and gardens adult £9, concessions £8, child £4, family £25.

Park and gardens adult £4, concessions £3.50, child £2.50.

Telephone 01833 660 202.

To reach Whitworth Hall take the A688 from the A1. Telephone 01388 811772.

Simonside

Stand on the crest at Lordenshaws hillfort in Northumberland and the Coquet Valley stretches out expansively below. Immediately behind the fort is the distinctive signature of the outline of the Simonside Hills and further to the left are the unmistakable contours of the Cheviots. It's powerful country.

For those who visit the area today, Lordenshaws and Simonside are special places. But then the evidence shows that they have been special for 5,000 years or more. The lure today is the tranquillity, sweeping views, nature and sense of space.

But another layer of interest is that history is everywhere on the ground, suggesting that the place was of great significance to ancient peoples. Scattered around Lordenshaws are examples of prehistoric cup and ring rock carvings, thought to be from between 5,000 and 4,000 years ago. Rock art occurs across upland areas of the region and its meaning is a mystery.

The best that can be said is that it is often found on trackways and in areas commanding views and may reflect the mobile lifestyle of its Neolithic creators. Theories abound, and include territorial markers, ways of identifying good hunting grounds, messages to people passing through, fertility symbols ...

Its use in Bronze Age burials indicates that the symbols may have had different meanings to later peoples. The rock art panels are often linked to Bronze Age burial cairns, and this is the case at Lordenshaws. The place drew Iron Age settlers who around 350BC built the ramparts and ditches of the hillfort. There are two entrances, with the eastern one being better preserved with some facing stones

Above: The restored 12th Century Brinkburn Priory.

Left: A modern carving in beech of The Risen Christ by sculptor Fenwick Lawson.

still in place. Each entrance is approached by a sunken trackway.

Around 500 years after its construction, when defences were no longer needed, part of the ramparts were cleared to create a site for stone roundhouses.

Just outside Rothbury lies Brinkburn Priory, a secluded and peaceful setting in a loop on the banks of the River Coquet. Visitors can wander in the grassed surrounds of the restored 12th Century priory and absorb the tranquil air of the place as the river bubbles by.

Today the priory is home to nursery roosts of Daubenton's, natterer, noctule, Brandt's, whiskered and pipistrelle bats.

After descending through a wooded dene, visitors are confronted by the Norman doorway of the church. Inside there are three tiers of triple lancet stained glass windows and a modern carving in beech of The Risen Christ by North-East sculptor Fenwick Lawson.

During the laying of a new floor, the tomb slab of William, Prior of Brinkburn and suffragan Bishop of Durham who died in 1484, was found.

The church organ, built in 1868, was presented by Tyneside industrialist Lord Armstrong.

Elements of the priory also survive as part of the early 19th Century adjacent mansion, which was extended by architect John Dobson in the 1830s.

The house, the home of the Cadogan family, has been unoccupied since 1952. The site is now in the care of English Heritage.

Andrew Miller was born and brought up within sight of Simonside and today lives at nearby Thropton.

"I have looked at Simonside virtually every day of my life and for the people of Rothbury, it is the horizon," he says.

"It can affect so many things, including the mood of the place. People feel that it is a very special place and has always been so.

"For local people that shape of Simonside means a lot and people who go up there find out what a fantastic history is present," says Andrew, who works as farming and land management team leader at Northumberland National Park.

It is, says Andrew, the first big hill which comes into the view of travellers on the A1 from Tyneside.

"It stands out. It has a presence, partly because of its shape and its position in the landscape and when the heather blooms it is alive with colour.

"None of these things have changed over the centuries."

The fort is surrounded by medieval rig and furrow plough markings and from the mid-14th Century was owned by the Percy family.

Running across the area is the boundary and remains of walls of a 13th Century deer park carved out by Robert FitzRoger, Lord of the Manor of Rothbury.

A short distance away is what survives of Tosson Tower, now a scheduled ancient monument, which was built as a stronghold by the Ogle family as Border conflict intensified 600 years ago. It is probably no accident that so much activity takes place over such a long period just beneath Simonside. It is thought by some experts that Simonside may have had sacred status.

The upper ridge of the hills mark them out as an important landmark and Simonside has been the subject of a project involving Forest Enterprise and the universities of Durham and Lancaster.

Finds of flints show that Mesolithic people from 10,000-6,000 years ago were active on Simonside. Bronze swords and rings have also been found. Concentrations of later burial cairns have been discovered just downhill from a feature called Little Church Rock.

This is an isolated and prominent outcrop of fell sandstone on the steep north-facing slope of Simonside, which also includes a cave.

It has been established

Simonside vista.

that 2,500 years after their construction, some of the cairns were re-used for the burial of warriors.

What is one of the most captivating historic landscapes in Northumberland National Park at Lordenshaws - only a couple of miles or so from Rothbury - is accessible thanks to an agreement between the park authority, the Duke of Northumberland and the tenant farmer.

Simonside can be explored through waymarked trails created by Forest Enterprise from its car park half a mile along the minor road from Lordenshaws.

They take in Little Church Rock, another rock shelter and criss-cross rock. This a flat sandstone which individuals are forced to walk on because of boulders on either side. The slab has been chiseled with sets of crossed lines, creating a grid pattern. The track was once a droveway and the grid may have been intended to stop cattle slipping as they climbed the hill.

But the markings may also be prehistoric.

The Cheviots, taken from Lordenshaws Hill Fort.

It is one of the many mysteries surrounding the two sites which continue to exercise their power over today's visitors. The trackways, carvings and cairns reflect thousands of years of human activity.

Lordenshaws and Simonside can be reached via Rothbury on the B6344. Take the bridge across the River Coquet and keep left to climb away from Rothbury on the B6342 until you take a right-hand turn at the Northumberland National Park sign.

The minor road is also marked by a brown sign for Simonside.

Off this road are car parks for Lordenshaws and Simonside.

The national park has produced a walks leaflet for Simonside.

Brinkburn Priory is open from March 24-September 30, 10am-6pm daily.

Admission is Adult £2.30, Concession £1.70 and Child £1.20. Telephone (01665) 570628.

Brinkburn Priory is 4.5 miles south-east of Rothbury off the B6344.

Belsay Hall and Gardens

Sir Charles Monck was not a man to do things by halves. For starters, his honeymoon lasted for six months.

After marrying in the less than exotic surrounds of Doncaster in 1804, he and his new wife visited Berlin, Dresden, Prague, Vienna, Trieste and Greece.

It was the classical and romantic aspects of Greece which made a big impact on Sir Charles, and on his return to his estate in Belsay in Northumberland,

he set about designing a grand country house on the lines of the ancient Temple of Theseus in Athens. The result is Belsay Hall, now in the care of English Heritage.

Sir Charles also extended the parkland to the south, and demolished the village of Belsay, building a new settlement well out of sight.

Work on the hall started in 1807 but it was not until Christmas Day in 1817 that he and his family moved in, although only the entrance hall and the bedroom above were

finished. They left behind their old residence in Belsay Castle, which dates from at least the mid-15th Century.

To make the castle fit into his newly-designed landscape, Sir Charles reduced the building almost to its 17th Century proportions. Today, the castle and hall are two of Belsay's main attractions.

But the real glory of Belsay is the beautiful and immaculately-tended gardens. The 30 acres of garden open to the public, described by English Heritage as "one of the

Belsay Hall has 30 acres of gardens open to the public.

most magnificent in Britain," form the core of Sir Charles's landscape around the hall. And it was Sir Charles who presided over what is Belsay's jewel.

The stone for Belsay Hall was quarried from the park with excavations being controlled so that they created a picturesque canyon through a hill, which connects the hall and castle. Sir Charles turned the rock corridor into a garden in the Romantic style, which with its sheltered micro-climate and exotic plants exercises its spell on all who visit. Due to its depth and a belt of yews and Scots pine on the north cliff, the windless Quarry Garden

The Belsay estate has belonged to the Middleton family since at least 1270. At that time it was owned by Sir Richard de Middleton, Lord Chancellor to Henry III.

Sir Charles Middleton took the name of Monck as a condition of his inheriting an estate in Lincolnshire from his maternal grandfather.

Sir Charles's grandson, Sir Arthur, resumed the name of Middleton in 1876. The estate was occupied by the family until 1962.

During the Second World War, Belsay was in the hands of the military.

The early Middletons built the castle tower during the time of Border warfare. In one of the rooms is a rare survivor, part of the painted plaster which once decorated all of its walls.

Believed to date from the 15th Century, the plaster images include a vine trellis pattern, trees, shields and ships.

An unfortified extension was added in 1614 in more peaceful times. There is also an ornamental folly called Castle Bantham, which had been built by the 18th Century.

Above: The Ornamental Garden at Belsay Hall.
Centre: The magnificent Quarry Garden at Belsay Hall.
Right: The Chusan Palm and stone archway in the Quarry Garden.

has a beguiling stillness and calmness.

The quarry is approached through a grove of Japanese cedars, and is home to a range of unusual plants, including an enkianthus bought in 1908 for seven shillings and six pence. Rhododendrons bloom alongside the skunk cabbage from the United States and native and exotic ferns.

A hollow off the main quarry is an environmentally sensitive zone of liverworts and mosses, while a spring-fed pond spreads into a bog garden.

Fronting a stone arch is an old Chusan palm tree whose trunk is wrapped in layers of its old leaves to protect it in winter. Beyond the arch the quarry opens into an area of cliff and rock pinnacles where more rhododendrons grow to up to 40ft.

"There isn't anything like the quarry garden in this country," says Belsay head gardener Paul Harrigan.

The Belsay gardens experience begins outside the hall itself. Terrace beds overlook masses of rhododendrons planted between 1904-30. The main flowering period, with hues of red, pink, mauve and white, is from late May to mid-June.

The route leads to the yew garden, the Magnolia Terrace, and the Winter Garden, with its 92ft Douglas Fir which was planted in 1830 – one of the first after its introduction into Britain from North America in 1827.

Paul and his team have also been building up a collection of lilies.

"We are aiming for more than 40 species flowering from mid-May until mid-September and reaching up to 10ft in the quarry," he says.

The Winter Garden faces a sunken croquet lawn, where a thriving croquet club plays. It is a special, time-warp experience to sit in the sunshine in this garden, with the background scents of flowers and birdsong

which merges with the dull "thwock" of croquet mallet on ball. Watching the white-clad players engage in a game which is quintessentially English country house from another age, and then to exit via a small wooden door in the garden wall, has more than a hint of Alice in Wonderland about it.

Belsay Hall, castle and gardens are 14 miles northwest of Newcastle on the A696, telephone (01661) 881636.

Opening times are March 24 – September 30, 10am-6pm, closing at 4pm from October 1 – March 31.

Admission adults £5.30 concessions £4, children £2.70, family ticket £13.30. There is a tearoom and shop.

There is also a leaflet walk featuring Crag

Wood and lake, which were created by Sir Charles in the early 19th Century.

Kielder Forest

So what is there more of in the North-East than anywhere else in England? Trees.

Kielder Forest Park in Northumberland and stretching into part of Cumbria is the largest forest in the country and one of the biggest man-made forests in Europe. It covers 150,000 acres between the Border and Hadrian's Wall, and contains an estimated 150 million trees.

The brief of the early foresters was simple - grow timber for Britain. The nation had been handed a warning during the First World War about how supplies from overseas could be cut off. The Forestry Commission bought an initial 2,000 acres at Smales Farm near Falstone in Northumberland and in 1926 the first tree was planted. The aim was to produce as high a volume of timber as quickly as possible by using fast-growing conifers.

Between the 1930s and 1960s, vast blankets of conifers, leaving little open space, gradually covered the moorland.

How times change. Today, although Kielder is still very much a working forest with 5,000 trees - equal to 1,000 tonnes of timber - being harvested every day the forest is now just as important for nature conservation and recreation.

Together with Kielder Water reservoir, the area is now the base for another industry - tourism - with 350,000 visitors a year. As the forest and the surrounds of Kielder Water

A view of Leaplish which caters for the needs of visitors to Kielder.

People as well as wildlife are increasingly benefiting from Kielder. The Forestry Commission has a policy of open access and there are more than 20 waymarked walks, cycle and horse trails. People are welcome to walk anywhere in the forest, subject to operational precautions. Walks range from the gentle, with the Duke's Trail at Kielder Castle including a one-mile section suitable for wheelchairs, to strenuous "classic" hikes.

The castle was built by the Duke of Northumberland in 1775 as a hunting lodge and now houses a visitor centre and is the focal point for trails.

Kielder campsite has a resident warden plus showers and toilets but 18 wilderness backpack sites are on offer where there is no vehicle access and the only facility is a stream.

The 12-mile route from Kielder Castle to one of the longest of place names in the region – Blakehopeburnhaugh – on the A68 is the longest forest toll road in Britain.

mature, they are softening and shading into a more natural-looking landscape. That process is being given a big helping hand by a programme of forest design plans and restructuring with the objective of changing the even-aged straight-line plantations to a more diverse forest.

One target is to create a variety of habitats for plants and wildlife. The restructuring includes developing a mosaic of areas of different-aged trees as blocks maturing after 40 to 50 years present the opportunity for change. Around 2,500 acres are felled every year and 2.7 million new trees are planted to provide a sustainable supply of timber. Each stage in the developing forest – bare

The origins of Kielder Forest can be traced to when Roy Robinson was asked by the Government to report on sites for growing timber for Britain. Kielder caught his eye and Lord Robinson, as he became, went on to be chairman of the Forestry Commission and witnessed the first tree planting 78 years ago. He returned in 1948 to fell the first tree. After his death in 1952 his ashes were scattered among the trees and his memorial cairn is at Whickhope in the forest.

In 1932 the Forestry Commission bought 50,000 acres and Kielder Castle from the Duke of Northumberland.

Land continued to be acquired until 1969, with half of the forest being planted from 1945-60 with memories of the Battle of the Atlantic attempts in the Second World War to snap UK supply lines still fresh.

Clearance of the last forest to cloak the area was started by prehistoric man. Evidence of man's activity from 6,000 years ago has been discovered at Plashetts, while the Devil's Lapful is a Bronze Age burial cairn from around 4,500 years ago near Kielder Castle.

By the mid-19th Century coal mining was under way at Lewisburn by landowner Sir John Swinburne, who built a road to transport the coal to market. The original toll stone showing the charges can still be seen at Bloodybush on what is now a cycle and horse trail.

In 50 years the creation of Kielder Forest wrought the most dramatic change which the landscape had seen for many centuries. But remarkably, this mammoth task was to be equalled – if not trumped – with the carving out of the giant Kielder Water reservoir.

was identified in 1993, making it the oldest recorded of its species in the country.

Mature trees are seed banks for crossbills and siskins, who in turn feed forest-nesting sparrowhawks and goshawks. The forest is also one of the last refuge in England for the red squirrel.

Restructuring means lines of trees following natural contours, more open space and an increase in native broadleaf tree planting from the original 1pc of the forest to 10pc. The 10pc figure may not sound much but it adds up to 12,500 acres of broadleaf trees, many along the 370 miles of watercourses in Kielder where the increased open space is taken over by meadow

ground, young and mature trees - offer different habitats for various wildlife species. Clear-felled land is recolonised by plant communities and becomes rich in insects and small mammals. They provide food for birds like kestrels and tawny owls.

As the trees grow to their middle years, they act as song posts for whinchats and warblers and home to goldcrests and coal tits. Around 6,000 roe deer benefit from the shelter and grass. To keep tree damage to an economic level 2,000 deer are culled annually.

Bats also find Kielder a good place to hang out. A pipistrelle bat ringed in 1980 near Kielder Castle

Kielder Castle

trees planted, with smaller numbers of other conifers such as Norway spruce, Scots pine, and lodgepole pine.

Bill Burlton, district environment forester, has watched the changes over the last 20 years.

He says: "The early stages of conifers are attractive to birds like the song thrush. We probably have more song thrushes in Kielder than there are in the rest of Northumberland."

The Forestry Commission has been working with Newcastle University on how to manage Kielder to benefit the red squirrel. This means dropping plans to plant large-seeded broadleaf trees like the oak, which grey squirrels prefer.

"Without Kielder it is questionable whether red

sweet, water avens, valerian, ragged robin, melancholy and marsh thistle. With 10pc given to broadleaf planting and 10pc to open space, a fifth of the forest will be non-conifer.

Around 450 species of plants, 175 of birds, and 600 of insects have been recorded at Kielder Forest Park, which is made up of the forests of Redesdale, Kielder, Falstone, Wark, Kershope and Spadeadam. Sitka spruce, which thrives in the northern upland areas, makes up 80pc of

Kielder Castle's Visitor Centre.

squirrels can survive in England," says Bill.

Another strategic decision has been to aid the recovery of the rare black grouse.

At present there are large areas where the moor and forest edge meet abruptly. The plan is to create 7,500 acres of mixed broadleaf and spruce moorland – a habitat in which the black grouse should do well.

More than 20 years of monitoring 250 tawny owl nest boxes and the pellets of the birds suggest that the forest is taking on a more mature character, as the birds' diet now includes more mammals such as wood mice and bank voles.

Kielder also has the internationally-important habitat of blanket bog, some up to 30ft deep. The

Border Mires and their plant and insect communities cover 4,000 acres and a survey by English Nature has pinpointed the bogs which existed before afforestation. Damage caused by forestry is being reversed, with 650 acres being cleared of trees so far and 8,000 dams inserted in old drainage channels to raise water levels. On dry hilltops, around 200 pools

have been created by using explosives to blast craters which fill with water. They generate insect food for the young of dunlin and golden plover.

In all there are 21 sites of special scientific interest at Kielder, covering 20,000 acres.

Bill says: "Kielder makes a major contribution to the North-East's biodiversity. The working forest brings money and jobs to the local economy but with careful planning we can mix forestry with conservation and recreation for people."

Kielder is reached from the A68 via the B6320. The route via Greenhaugh takes in expansive moorland vistas.

An alternative is to take the B6320 to Wark from the A69.

Kielder Castle visitor centre is open daily from April to October from 10am-5pm and November to December at weekends only 11am-4pm. The centre includes forest and birdlife exhibitions, an art gallery, the Duke's Pantry cafe, toilets, and details on walks and cycle hire. Telephone 01434 250 209.

Kielder Village has a youth hostel which is the only one in England to be awarded five stars for quality. Telephone 01434 250 195.

Pubs include the Pheasant Inn and restaurant 01434 240 382, the Blackcock Inn at Falstone 01434 240 200 and the Anglers Arms at Kielder 01434 250 072.

Kielder Water

North Tyne Valley dwellers like Janet Scott watched over the years as the planting of millions of conifers to create Kielder Forest slowly changed the landscape. But for Janet and the rest of the close community in the Kielder area, an even more profound transformation was in the pipeline.

Experts were watching demand for water rise from industry and domestic customers, whose changing lifestyles now embraced washing machines, dishwashers, showers, garden sprinklers and car washes.

To meet this thirst for more water, the decision was made to build the biggest man-made lake in northern Europe.

The chosen site was Kielder in Janet Scott's North Tyne Valley, where she has lived for more than 50 years.

Work started in 1975, with up to 1,500 construction workers pouring into the remote rural area.

The Queen opened the fruits of their labour, Kielder reservoir, in 1982.

A total of 1.5million trees were felled and big farms such as Mounces Hall and Otterslee were demolished to make way for the water, while another 70 homes and the winding road of the valley were submerged. The result was a lake covering 2,700 acres and holding 44,000 million gallons, with a shoreline of 27 miles.

Today, together with Kielder Forest, the reservoir is a man-made landscape which, as it ages, looks deceptively natural and attracts hundreds of thousands of holidaymakers, day visitors and recreational users every year.

At the same time, both forest and lake deliver the fundamental commodities of wood and water, with tourism an added economic benefit.

Left: Kielder Water is a man-made reservoir built over 7 years.

Right: Kielder Viaduct on Kielder Water.

Water from Kielder flows into the Tyne and can be transferred to the Wear and the Tees and – in emergencies – to Yorkshire. It is part of the UK's first example of a regional water grid.

The search for a major new reservoir was sparked by anticipated soaring demand for water from industry, especially on Teesside. After ICI decided in the 1950s to build its huge complex at Wilton on Teesside, Selset, Balderhead and Cow Green reservoirs were built. That meant the Tees Valley could not accommodate any further water storage developments.

Four options were examined to provide more water – a tidal barrage, a plant to convert sea water, tapping water-bearing rock strata, and a reservoir. A reservoir was the choice and 38 sites were investigated.

The chosen one was upstream from Falstone, where a dam could be built at one of the narrowest parts of the North Tyne Valley. The site contained sand, gravel, rock and boulder clay, deposited by glaciers 15,000 years ago, and which could be used in the construction. The creation of the £167m reservoir was a prodigious feat.

The valve tower, which releases water from the reservoir, is taller than Nelson's Column, yet it was built in 10 days using a continuous concrete-pouring process.

Two hydro-electric generators in the dam use water releases to produce sufficient power to illuminate a town the size of Hexham. But the anticipated industrial demand for water did not happen, which led to "white elephant" claims. But Kielder has since turned into a trump card for the region – especially with climate change – which can be used to attract companies looking for guaranteed water supplies.

Water to be switched to the Wear or Tees is taken from the Tyne at Riding Mill in Northumberland, where the biggest pumping station of its type in the UK helps supplies along their way through 20 miles of tunnels beneath County Durham. They can carry up to 250m gallons a day.

Amid all this the salmon and their lost North Tyne spawning grounds were not forgotten. The Kielder salmon hatchery produces many thousands of juvenile fish to stock the Tyne and rivers further afield.

Kielder Maze.

Janet has run a bed-and-breakfast business from her home overlooking the lake for 35 years. Her father was a shepherd in the area and her husband John was Kielder postman for 45 years.

Of the pre-flood community, she says: "It was small and happy. We were content with very little."

A setback was the closure of the Border Counties railway line through Kielder.

"That was a sad day," Janet says. But the planting of the forest pushed steadily on and then came the flooding.

The task of developing Kielder as a major sustainable tourism asset is the job of the Kielder Partnership.

The ace in the pack for the partnership is the Kielder sculpture trail, with works at the water's edge and in the forest in what is essentially an open air gallery. There are 13 artworks. They range from Waterstones, erected in 1982 with the stones being cut from a quarry near Elsdon, to

James Turrell's Skyspace, a contemplative chamber where the visitor's attention is focused on the sky through an opening in the roof, and the award-winning Belvedere shelter and Minotaur maze.

Partnership officer Paul Nichol says: "The sculptures add interest and broaden the appeal of Kielder. They draw in new audiences and provide a focus point for walks."

"It is unbelievable the way things have changed. It is just amazing.

"I knew every inch of ground which is under the water and it is sad to see places you knew disappear like that and be gone forever."

But the forest and the lake have brought jobs which were not there before and what was once an alien reservoir has now become familiar. Janet says: "It looks quite a natural setting now and I have wonderful views from the house over the lake.

"I have met many foreign visitors through the B&B. It makes life interesting."

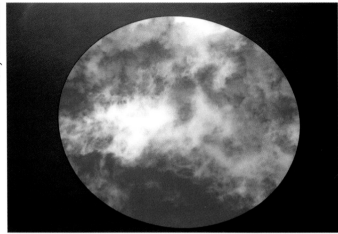

The view from the Skyspace sculpture at Kielder.

Janet's daughter, Ellen Earsman, is one who has benefited from the new economy of the North Tyne Valley. She is a team leader who looks after the visitor accommodation at Kielder for Northumbrian Water.

Ellen, 55, who lives at Stannersburn at the mouth of Kielder Water, says: " It was a picturesque valley even before the reservoir came. I remember the twisty road through the trees.

"Now most of the places I remember are under water.

"There were very mixed feelings about the reservoir when it was proposed. Some were dead against it."

But Ellen, who had two daughters, took comfort in the belief that it would bring work for youngsters who, if they did not find or want jobs in farming and forestry, would be forced to leave the area. It was Ellen's daughter Sheena who, on her 12th birthday, presented a bouquet to the Queen at the reservoir opening ceremony.

Ellen says: "I think I have grown with the lake. To me it now feels like it has been there forever."

Tonia Reeve, who lives in nearby Bellingham, remembers being given the day off school for the Queen's visit and being bussed to Leaplish on the lake shoreline for the event.

"It was just a rough forest road and a wooden hut," says Tonia, now commercial operations manager for Northumbrian Water based at Leaplish. Today, Leaplish has 32 holiday log cabins, a bunk barn, restaurant, bar and shop, indoor pool and

Nature has a special place at Bakethin on Kielder Water. The Bakethin Dam was built at the shallow, north-western end of Kielder Water. This was to prevent the appearance of unsightly mudflats which would otherwise be exposed when water levels dropped in the main reservoir.

Bakethin lake – which covers 155 acres – and its surrounds are a designated nature conservation area. A bird hide has been provided and artificial islands and otter holts built. To encourage otters, young eels have been released to bulk up food supplies. Northumbrian Water funds the post of a wetlands conservation officer at Bakethin who works for Northumberland Wildlife Trust.

sauna, conference centre, bird of prey centre, camping and caravan sites, and is a departure point for the ferry Osprey, which takes visitors on lake cruises. Visitors come to walk, cycle, sail, water ski and fish.

Tonia says: "Comments from the majority of people are that they come for the peace, tranquillity, fresh air, to get out of the cities and to chill out.

"Now many places don't look man made, but seem

Sunset over Kielder Water.

very natural. People are taken aback by the scenery."

For the majority of people, first call is the Tower Knowe visitor centre with its exhibition on the Kielder story, restaurant, and shops.

David Hall, Northumbrian Water commercial and leisure business manager, says: "Kielder is a strategic water asset."

But the leisure side of the business is virtually stand alone and pays its way, at peak times providing up to 70 jobs.

David says: "We plan to grow the business in a sensible way and have commissioned a study which explores the further potential of Kielder."

The Tower Knowe visitor centre is open daily from April and October from 10am-4pm, May, June and September to 5pm and July and August to 6pm.

There is the Kielder Water exhibition, gift, souvenir and fishing tackle shop, Osprey ferry point, picnic sites, self-guided trails and a restaurant. Telephone: (01434) 240436.

Leaplish Waterside Park has a lakeside restaurant and bar, shop, indoor pool and sauna, conference centre, ferry point, bird of prey centre, picnic site, waymarked walks and cycle routes, artworks, forest lodges, a bunkhouse, caravan and camping sites.

Telephone: (0870) 2403549.

Kielder Castle visitor centre includes exhibitions, shop, and a cafe. Telephone: (01434) 250209.

The 80-seat ferry Osprey operates from April to October 31. Adults £5.25, OAP £4.75, children £3.

Kielder Bikes offer cycle hire. Telephone: (01434) 250392.

View of Durham Cathedral from Crook Hall.

Durham

A thousand years of history underpins the world heritage site city of Durham, dating from the arrival of the body of St Cuthbert in 995. The cathedral, castle, the museums, leafy riverside walks, botanic gardens all vie for the visitor's attention.

But a five-minute walk from the Market Place is a gem which is easily overlooked amid all the heavyweight attractions. The medieval Crook Hall and its satellite gardens are an enchanting find.

Keith and Maggie Bell are the latest in a long line of occupants at Crook Hall, which is a rare survivor of a small medieval manor house. The hall encapsulates the development of English domestic architecture over four centuries.

Fortunately, when tastes and requirements changed, the hall was not knocked down but was added to with Jacobean and Georgian additions which widen its Grade I listed charms.

Visitors approach through a meadow area, where Keith and Maggie are developing a maze, and turn into the Secret Garden. This is a walled garden of old rose varieties, fruit trees and magnolias. The garden was visited by William and Dorothy Wordsworth and the Lake District writer and artist John Ruskin, who were friends of the then-occupant, the historian Dr James Raine.

While much of Durham's charm is in its architecture, Durham University's 18-acre botanic garden offers a contrasting pleasure. The first treat for visitors is the Prince Bishops Garden, designed as Durham County Council's contribution to the 1990 National Garden Festival at Gateshead. The botanic garden's cornflower annual border aims to recreate the kind of wild flower display common in arable fields before the introduction of modern herbicides. Herbicides can deplete the flower seed bank in the soil in farmland. But the border is repeatedly sown with corn chamomile, corn marigold, corn cockle, corn flower and corn poppy. It also has examples of some of the world's most endangered trees. There is the spindle tree, a hedgerow species with crimson autumn foliage and fruits like dangling pink lanterns. It has been cut down in many places because it is a winter host to black bean aphid which attacks broad bean crops.

Durham has its monkey puzzle tree – a tree which has outlived the dinosaurs, and a beech tree which bears 170,000 leaves in summer.

Its water consumption is equal to the contents of 10 car petrol tanks an hour – illustrating how plants play a key part in regulating climate. Even a sunflower uses 17 times more water than a human every day.

The foxglove tree is also acting as an indicator of climate change. Bud burst, flowering, and leaf colour change are sensitive to weather shifts which may be linked to global warming. The tree is at the limit of its climatic tolerance in Durham. For 10 years it struggled to survive, but in 2001 it flowered for the first time.

Displays of rosemary, lavender and bay show how flavours and scents have led people to use them as food additives and perfumes.

Plants contain an enormous range of natural chemicals and, although 40pc of the medicines in a chemist's shop have natural plant extracts, so far only a fraction of what is on offer in nature has been identified and exploited.

Indoor attractions include the cactus house, tropical house, and a conservatory housing tropical bugs including preying mantis, stick insects and tarantula spiders.

Crook Hall, Durham.

Go through a wrought-iron gate and a second walled garden opens up, packed with cottage garden flowers which frame the hall buildings.

The Billingham family lived at Crook Hall for around 300 years until 1657. Roof timbers have been dated to 1467-68 and the hall contains what are perhaps the oldest stairs in the city.

It also has a ghost, the White Lady, who has been the subject of numerous sightings.

Hooks in the beams of the hall were used by John Fowler for his beer-bottling business in the 1800s and some of his hops are still grown in the gardens.

Refreshments are served in the Georgian dining room

Walk along the banks of the River Wear in Durham and enjoy one of the great sights of Europe.

Stand opposite Durham Cathedral and its towers rear over the trees on the other side of the river. You have confirmation that this is, indeed, a world heritage site and why writer Bill Bryson described the cathedral as the finest building on Earth. This magnificent creation was built as a shrine to St Cuthbert and as a place for pilgrims, with the foundation stone being laid in 1093. The tomb of St Cuthbert lies at the east end of the cathedral. A Treasures of St Cuthbert exhibition includes the remains of the coffin in which he was placed in 698 and the cross found when his tomb was excavated in 1827.

It is the Venerable Bede we have to thank for what we know about St Cuthbert. Bede is buried in the cathedral's Galilee Chapel, begun in the 12th Century at the opposite end of the building to St Cuthbert.

Different aspects of the cathedral will catch different eyes.

For me, one of the most impressive sights is the huge clock in the South Transept, installed by Prior Thomas Castell in the 15th Century, which shows the time of day, day of the month and the phases of the Moon.

There are memorials to County Durham's miners and the Durham Light Infantry.

Behind the High Altar is the fabulous Neville Screen, given by the powerful family of the same name in the 14th Century. Before the Reformation the screen held 107 statues. It is believed they were hidden to prevent their destruction by the King's commissioners, but were never been re-discovered. The scale is breathtaking. Even in the monks' dormitory, each roof beam is constructed from a single oak tree.

or a peaceful flagged courtyard, and then it is on to another series of gardens.

The Cathedral Garden, with hedges cut with shapes reflecting ecclesiastical windows, offers views of Durham's skyline. The Silver Garden was planted with white and silver specimens for the silver wedding anniversary of previous occupants Dr and Mrs Hawgood. Elizabethan plants are a feature of the Shakespeare Garden and there is also the orchard. The fish-filled moat pond has been created by Keith and Maggie at the spot where, it is believed, a moat once existed. The combination of hall, history and horticulture is captivating.

Keith, the grandson of a Chopwell miner and Maggie, a Cumbrian farmer's daughter, met at Durham University. The couple bought Crook Hall in 1995.

"There is a magical feel about the place, with all its little hidden corners," says Maggie. "Through the centuries there have been a lot of gifted gardeners here and we have also developed the gardens."

The couple decided to open Crook Hall and gardens during afternoons after they received many requests to do so.

"We know we are only the custodians of the hall for a short time – the blink of an eye in the history of the place," says Maggie.

"Opening to the public helps us to look after the hall and preserve it for future generations."

Crook Hall is open 1pm-5pm on Easter weekend, Bank Holiday weekends and Sundays in May and September.

It is open daily in June, July and August and at Halloween, October 31, from 4pm-dusk.

Adults £4, concessions £3.50, family ticket £12. Tel: (0191) 384 8028.

The hall is located across the footbridge near Durham's tourist information centre.

Durham University Botanic Garden in Hollingside Lane is open every day from March to October from 10am-5pm and daily from November to February 10am-4pm.

Adults £2, concessions £1.50, children 5-16 and students £1. Tel: (0191) 334 5521.

Durham Cathedral is open Monday-Saturday 9.30am-6.15pm, Sunday 12.30pm-5pm with evening opening to 8pm from June 17-September 8.

Cathedral open for worship and private prayer Monday-Saturday 7.30am-9.30am, Sundays 7.45am-12.30pm. Chapter Office tel: (0191) 386 4266.

The book and gift shop in the Great Kitchen, part of the medieval priory, is open Monday to Saturday 9am-5.30pm, November until February 9am-5pm. Tel: (0191) 386 2972.

The cathedral restaurant is open Monday to Saturday 10am-5pm, Sunday 10.30am-5pm. Closes 4.30pm mid-October to late May. Tel: (0191) 386 3721.

Durham Castle is open July to September and Easter and Christmas vacations daily 10am-12.30pm and 2pm-4.30pm.

Other times of year: Monday, Wednesday, Saturday, Sunday 2pm-4pm.

Adults £5, concessions £2.50, children £2.50, family ticket £10. Tel: (0191) 334 3800.

Other attractions include Old Fulling Mill Museum of Archaeology, tel: (0191) 334-1823; Durham Light Infantry Museum and Durham Art Gallery, tel: (0191) 384 2214; Durham University Oriental Museum (0191) 334 5694; Durham Heritage Centre (0191) 384- 5589; Gala Theatre (0191) 332 4041.

Dunstanburgh Castle

When it comes to majestic settings, Bamburgh Castle would take some topping.

Yet if we journey only a short distance south along the Northumbrian coast, there is a sight which, for many people, does just that. The view from Embleton Bay across the water to the ruins of Dunstanburgh Castle sitting on its 100ft cliffs, is arguably one of the finest in Britain. It is the most romantic and dramatic of images.

No doubt that is how Thomas Earl of Lancaster envisaged it as he chose the coastal headland in the early 14th Century for the site his castle on which he spared no expense.

A beautiful sunrise overlooking Dunstanburgh Castle.

After becoming militarily redundant in the mid-15th Century, Dunstanburgh Castle returned briefly to "active service" more than 500 years later.

Access to the castle is via a one-and-a-half-mile coastal walk from the village of Craster. This stretch was recently the subject of an archaeological investigation by English Heritage, which manages the castle, and the National Trust, which owns it.

What it revealed was the role played by this part of the shoreline in the Second World War, when Embleton Bay was seen as a potential landing beach for the Germans. Fear of invasion saw a detachment of the Royal Armoured Corps base itself amid the ruins. The area was also the site of a top-secret radar station which was part of the Battle of Britain defences. The archaeologists located about 30 machine gun positions and weapon pits, where a minefield had been positioned, and pill boxes. In 1944 the radar site was used to house Italian Prisoners of War, who built Mediterranean-style terrace gardens, the remains of which survive today.

The setting entranced the great JMW Turner who visited in 1797. One of his paintings, showing the rugged setting of the castle and its wild seascape, was bought by the Laing Art Gallery in Newcastle.

The puzzle of Dunstanburgh is – what is it supposed to be defending? There is no river crossing, the Border is 25 miles away, and it is some way off the main north-south road.

Dunstanburgh is now increasingly being seen as a "show castle", built to magnify the power and the standing of Earl Thomas, leader of England's barons who were not exactly enamoured of Edward II.

Thomas was the greatest man in the realm after his cousin, the king, and in 1315 was commander of the royal forces in the north.

Dunstanburgh was built to reflect his status and probably to trump Bamburgh, which was indirectly a royal fortress.

Recent archaeological work has uncovered evidence that the castle, with its elegant towers, was surrounded by ornamental lakes.

A painting of Dunstanburgh Castle by JMW Turner.

It was to Dunstanburgh that Thomas and his followers began to retreat after an abortive rebellion against the king.

But they were intercepted in Yorkshire and defeated. The Earl was executed, leaving an enduring legacy to the Northumbrian coastline. And a lavish legacy it is. The castle encloses 11 acres - more than any other Northumbrian fortress.

This would have provided room for the tenants of Earl Thomas, who was lord of Embleton, and their livestock in times of danger.

The most impressive aspect of the castle is the early 14th Century gatehouse.

On an income of £11,000 a year - a fortune in those times - the Earl wanted a gatehouse in the latest fashion and that was what

Right: Beadnell Beach.

he got. He paid £280 to the mason in charge, Master Elias. Just how much that was can be judged by the fact that farming labourers earned one and a half pence a day.

Later, the castle became the property of John of Gaunt, son of Edward III. He decided to revamp Dunstanburgh, partly to accommodate his followers. There were plenty of them. When he came to the Border to negotiate a truce with the Scots in 1380, his retinue totalled 2,000 men.

The castle was besieged in 1462 during the Wars of the Roses by a Yorkist force. Starvation forced the garrison to surrender after it had eaten its horses.

By the mid-16th Century, Dunstanburgh verged on the ruinous, with only 72s 8d (£3.64p) being spent on repairs.

Finally, the castle came into the hands of Newcastle shipowner Sir Arthur Sutherland, who in 1929 gave it to the Office of Works, which was the forerunner of English Heritage.

Dunstanburgh Castle is eight miles North-East of Alnwick by footpaths from Craster and Embleton.

It is open from April 1-September 30 10am-6pm daily; October 1-30 10am-4pm daily; November 2-March 31 10am-4pm Thursday-Monday.

Admission adults £2.60, concessions £2, children £1.30.

Tel: (01665) 576231.

Farne Islands

The Farne Islands off Northumberland are forever linked with St Cuthbert. As such, they were a place of pilgrimage for centuries.

Today, most of the 32,000 visitors a year to the National Trust islands are on a pilgrimage of a different kind.

They go to enjoy the spectacular sight of masses of nesting birds which the Trust describes as "one of the most exciting wildlife experiences in the world." The count hovers at around 100,000 nesting pairs, and then there is the 3,500-strong seal colony.

But perhaps the pilgrimage is not so different after all.

For St Cuthbert, who lived on the islands, drew up rules for the welfare of eider ducks – now known as Cuddy's Ducks after the saint – during the breeding season.

According to John Walton, Trust property manager for the Farne Islands and stretches of the Northumbrian coastline, there are 15 islands at high tide and 28 at low tide. Birds breed on 12 of the islands.

Above: Longstone Lighthouse at Farne Islands.

Left: A tern takes an interest in a Farne Island visitor.

The islands consist of two main groups – Inner and Outer Farne – separated by the mile-wide Staple Sound.

The main island, Inner Farne, is more than 16 acres. The islands are the most easterly outcrop of the Great Whin Sill, the hard dolerite rock on which part of Hadrian's Wall is also built.

Island cliffs topping 20 metres in places and the deeply fissured rock provide excellent nesting sites.

But it's not all rock. There are three sandy beaches and boulder clay and peat on Brownsman, Staple Island, Inner Farne and West Wideopens accommodate plants. Surprisingly, 116 species of plants have been recorded, including the white-flowered sea campion, thrift, scurvy grass, ragwort, silverweed and a borage which originates from California and probably found its way to the islands in feed from the days when the lighthouse keepers kept poultry.

But it is the birds which are the stars of the islands.

"There are very few places in England where you would get that variety of seabirds," says John, who lives in Seahouses.

He worked as a cashier for Lloyds Bank in Newcastle before opting for a change of career and spending five seasons as a warden on the islands.

"I decided to follow my instincts," he says.

Nine wardens live on the islands between March and September and six from September to December. Their quarters are an old lighthouse keeper's cottage and a pele tower.

One of their jobs is to look after visitors and help the trust balance the needs of the birds with the people traffic. Visitors are allowed to land on Staple Island in the morning and Inner Farne in the afternoon, giving the birds 21 hours of peace.

The wardens also monitor bird and seal populations and on nest-counting days can be on the go from dawn until 8pm.

Several companies offer boat trips from Seahouses harbour. They include two-and-a-half hour trips with an hour landing, cruises around the islands and fishing and diving outings.

It is estimated that the Farne Islands bring £2m a year in visitor spending to the local economy, which was once centred on fishing.

Billy Shiel has been ferrying passengers to the islands for 60 years.

He says: "Tourism is important to the local economy.

"There is still a bit of fishing going on but I have

The puffin is the main player on the Farne Islands. The burrowing birds are also known as the sea parrot because of their brightly-coloured beaks, and Farne birds can live for more than 20 years. Monitoring of the bird populations by the island wardens shows a puffin population of more than 50,000 pairs.

The total number of bird species observed on the islands stands at 291. The ringing of birds on the Farne Islands reveals the travels and fates of individuals. Sandwich terns from the islands, which migrate to West Africa, have been found in Namibia, Guinea Bissau and Gambia. Six Farne Islands sandwich terns were also recorded at a major breeding colony off the Jutland peninsula in Denmark.

An Arctic tern ringed on Inner Farne was found dead near Durban in South Africa and another – at least 25 years old – died at Varmland in Sweden.

A kittiwake from the Farne Islands was shot dead in the Davis Strait, Greenland, where the birds are hunted.

There are also sightings from the islands of harbour porpoise, Minke whale and dolphin.

Seals have been on the Farne Islands for at least 800 years. The pups are born in October and November but of the average 1,200 new pups, between 50pc and 60pc die within three weeks, mainly due to weather conditions. Pups have been found, often when very young, in Norway, Sweden, Germany and Holland.

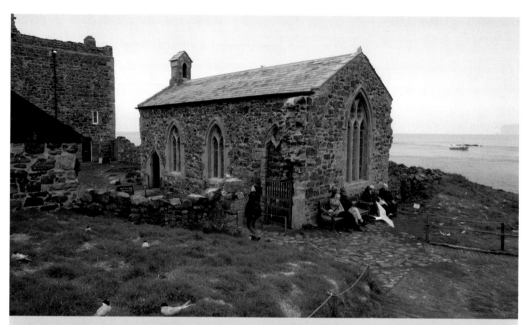

Hermits and monks lived on Inner Farne for nearly 900 years.

After serving for 12 years as Prior of Lindisfarne, St Cuthbert retired to Inner Farne from 678 to 684 when he became Bishop of Lindisfarne. In 686, he returned to Inner Farne, where he died on March 20, 687.

In 1246, a small daughter community of the convent of Durham was established called the House of Farne.

The present St Cuthbert's chapel was built in 1370 and was refurbished by Charles Thorp, Archdeacon of Durham, in 1861.

By then, exploitation of the seabirds was threatening the colonies and the Archdeacon employed wardens during the breeding season.

He furnished the chapel with 17th Century woodwork which had been removed from Durham Cathedral in 1848.

The island's tower was built in 1500 and in 1673 was the first official lighthouse when a fire was lit nightly on its top. The Longstone lighthouse was built in 1826 and was where sea rescue heroine Grace Darling's grandfather and father were keepers. In 1925, the islands were handed over to the National Trust.

seen big changes and now it is at an all-time low, unfortunately.

"The islands are saturated with wildlife.

"On a fine day you get people saying that the islands are fantastic, brilliant, stunning, because of all the wildlife."

The best views of the Farne Islands are from Bamburgh and Seahouses, which are reached via the B1342 from the A1 or the B1340 following the coastal route.

Boat trips leave from Seahouses, weather permitting.

National Trust landing charges are free for National Trusts members but non members a charge is payable to the Wardens on landing.

There are toilets on Inner Farne, an information centre and shop.

Telephone (01665) 721 099.

Alnwick Garden

As 1950 dawned it looked like the end of a great gardening era.

The glasshouses at Alnwick Castle's garden were dismantled and the land was turned into a tree nursery.

It was a sad and muted end to a gardening tradition which had started in the 18th Century as Capability Brown landscaped the parkland around the castle and the First Duke and Duchess laid the foundations for the beginning of the gardens.

Then in 1996 Jane, the Twelfth Duchess, embarked on a hugely ambitious venture to create a new and innovative garden within the walls of the old gardens.

Her vision was to fashion a garden that would be accessible to everyone and which would be a place of contemplation, fun, inspiration and education.

She brought on board Belgian landscape designer Jacques Wirtz and son Peter.

Of the garden site, Peter said: " It was a place of rubble, garden junk, ruinous building leftovers, soil storage and wilderness."

Today, the transformation has been so complete and so successful that the garden is on course for 600,000 visitors a year.

Yet an independent economic study had estimated that the garden would receive up to 230,000 visitors in the year in the year from April 2003 to March 2004.

In fact, 530,000 people arrived in 2003. So what was - and is - the big attraction?

In October 2001 the first phase of the 40-acre Alnwick Garden opened with the Grand Cascade as the centrepiece, plus ornamental and rose

gardens, and a woodland walk.

Over a million visitors later, this year the garden opened its second phase of developments.

This includes the tree house, poison garden, bamboo labyrinth and serpent garden.

A third phase, which will see the garden complete

between 2008-10, covers a visitor centre and pavilion, one of the largest "safely dangerous" playgrounds in Europe and a sophisticated lighting scheme which will interact with the water features.

In 2002 Prince Charles officially opened the garden and an independent charity, the Alnwick Garden Trust, was

set up to ensure the project works for the benefit of the North-East.

With the gardens run as a charity, all proceeds are used to maintain and administer the attraction and to finance future development.

The eyecatcher as the visitor enters the garden is, inevitably, the Grand Cascade which is one of the biggest water features of its kind in the UK.

The cascade, which uses stone from West Woodburn in Northumberland, has a series of 21 weirs down which tumbles 7,260 gallons of water a minute at peak flow.

The computer-controlled display changes sequence every 30 minutes, with four sequences in all.

Three large central jets reach a height of six metres, 40 smaller jets project water four metres into air and 80 side jets add to the show.

Underground, 250,000 gallons are stored and are filtered and recirculated.

A total of 850 hornbeam trees line the walks alongside the cascade.

At the top of the cascade is the ornamental walled

Although only half-complete in 2003, the Alnwick Garden attracted £13m in visitor spending from outside the North-East

It was also the third most visited paid for garden attraction in the UK after Kew and Wisley.

It is anticipated that, when complete, the

project will generate £150m in economic benefits for Northumberland over 10 years.

In 2003, 52% of visitors were from outside the region and they spent an average of £45 per trip.

On average, 600 garden visitors a day go on to look around the town.

In 2005 the Duchess, a trustee of the Alnwick Garden Trust, won the national award for outstanding contribution to tourism in the Enjoy England Excellence Awards.

garden, which is entered through three interlocked stone arches.

There are also 500-year-old wrought iron Venetian gates, bought by the 19th Century Fourth Duke who was fond of things Italian.

Another historic feature can be found on the edge of the rose garden in the shape of an 18th Century lead sculpted urn, with a fox sitting on top of the fruit-filled vessel which is decorated with masks depicting the four seasons and supported by monkeys.

The sculpture was bought by the Fourth Duke with the winnings from a bet on the horses.

The ornamental garden walls shelter the colours and scents of 16,500 plants in the flower and fruit collections.

The walls were built from bricks which arrived in Englad as ships' ballast and also support two dovecotes as well as climbers.

The rose garden is a perfumed treat of 3,000 rose bushes and climbers. One of the garden's sponsors, David Austin Roses, is behind the garden and in 2001 at the Chelsea Flower Show unveiled a new rich pink English rise called The Alnwick Garden.

In all, there are 65,000 individual plants in phase

Before construction of the Alnwick Garden began, 30 archaeologists worked for six weeks on a survey which revealed evidence of the remains of six previous gardens.

After the First Duke and Duchess started the ball rolling, the gardens at Alnwick began a century of development.

Hothouses were built to grow exotic produce such as pineapples, fuelled by coal from the Duke's mine at nearby Shilbottle.

In 1811 a gardener's cottage was built. The head gardener had a staff of 20.

The Third Duke was a plant collector who imported specimens and seeds from across the world to be grown at Alnwick.

He built a large conservatory in the gardens, and opened them on one day a week to the public.

He also had quite a taste for his Alnwick pineapples.

Produce from the hothouses was sent by main coach to the Duke in London and pineapples were despatched to Paris where he served as special ambassador in 1825 and Dublin where he was Lord Lieutenant in 1829-30.

Alnwick was acquiring a growing reputation for its gardens and in the 19th Century its head gardener was head hunted by Czar Alexander I.

The Fourth Duke added an Italianate garden and by the end of the 19th Century the gardens had topiary yew hedges, a double avenue of limes, acres of flower gardens, five grapehouses, five pinehouses, an a conservatory.

But two world wars, with the loss of manpower and the need for all available land to grow food, signalled the end of gardens on such a scale.

one of the garden, making it one of the largest European plant collections in the UK.

The opening of the tree house marked the start of 2005, with the 6,000 sq ft complex linked by walkways and offering a shop, eating places and decked veranda.

The treehouse was followed by the poison garden, telling the story of plants which have killed and cured, and the serpent garden, where steel and glass sculptures are used to illustrate how water behaves and moves.

The labyrinth has been planted with a variety of bamboo which can withstand winter temperatures of -20C.

Phase three envisages a garden of the senses, a spiral garden, grotto, quiet garden, and an orchard of 350 Tai Haku cherry trees.

The visitor centre and pavilion will include a gift and garden shop, a café with views over the cascade, exhibition, performance and functions spaces and education and interpretation areas where people can learn about the garden and the region.

It is being built on the site of the garden's 19th Century pavilion.

The charity is fund raising to pay for the projected

projects. The play area, accessible to wheelchair users, will cost around £3m-£5m and the lighting £2m.

The lighting infrastructure is in place and such a system would be an added attraction and an impetus to keep the garden open later at night, It would also be a winter bonus as it plays on the water and in colder spells, the ice.

Lighting on flexible rubber stakes could also be

planted to move and sway among the bamboo of the labyrinth.

The Duchess says: "The garden means different things to different people. I love the sound of children in the garden. It is a place for people.

"The garden is not about me. From day one it has been a public garden."

Alnwick Garden opening times are April to May 10am-6pm, June-September 10am-7pm, October 10am-6pm, November-January 10am 4pm, February-March 10am-5pm.

The admission ticket allows visitors to come and go throughout the day of purchase.

Admission: adult £6, over 60s and students £5.75.

Accompanied children under 16 are free with a maximum of three children per paying adult.

Telephone 01665 511 350.

South Shields

Left and top right:
Reconstructed Commanders
House at the Ardeia fort.

Above: Arbeia fort, South
Shields.

Slap bang amid the buzz of 21st-Century Tyneside is the imprint of a vastly different way of life from almost 2,000 years ago. On the densely-populated north and south banks of the River Tyne are two major Roman forts which have been coaxed back into existence after being hidden for centuries beneath fields and housing.

Arbeia fort at South Shields in South Tyneside was crucial as a supply base for the garrisons along Hadrian's Wall and as a gateway to the northern frontier of the Roman Empire.

Segedunum fort at Wallsend in North Tyneside was just as vital because of its position at the very eastern end of the Wall. The longest-running and most intense excavations of any Roman site in Britain – plus ambitious reconstruction of buildings – rescued the forts and deliver a vivid impression for visitors of life on Roman Tyneside.

An annual reminder comes in the shape of Roman coins which are washed up on the Herd Sands at South Shields. They are thought to be from a wrecked Roman ship which is still waiting to be discovered. Over the past century, a number of military items have been dredged from the river mouth, which add to the conviction that a wreck and its cargo are out there.

Research into the objects by archaeologist Paul Bidwell, who is based at Arbeia, suggest the wreck may date from the time of

The reconstructed gatehouse at Arbeia.

the Emperor Commodus, who featured as the villain in the film Gladiator.

Arbeia stands on the Lawe Top, a hill which would have offered views over the river mouth and out to sea. "The fort had an important role in guarding a harbour or port which has yet to be found," says Arbeia archaeologist Nick Hodgson.

Also awaiting discovery is the first fort at South Shields, which is believed to have been built in about AD125 beyond the current Arbeia site.

In about AD158 a new fort was constructed on four acres on the Lawe Top to house 480 infantry and 120 cavalry.

Fifty years later most of the buildings were demolished and replaced with 13 granaries as the fort increased in size, when the garrison was the Fifth Cohort of Gauls. The fort was now serving as a supply base, not least for the Scottish campaigns of the Emperor Severus from 208-211. Lead baggage seals, showing Severus and his sons Caracalla and Geta, have been found at South Shields, indicating that at some point they were based at the fort.

Nick says: "People tend to think of the Roman army using roads for transport, which they did, but they also used the sea and rivers where they could and which would have been quick and economical."

In the late Third to early Fourth Century, the fort was attacked and burned down. The rebuild saw granaries converted into barracks.

A Fourth-Century garrison was the Tigris Bargemen, originally raised in what is now Iraq, and one theory is that the name of Arbeia means "the place of the Arabs".

Nick says: "They were likely to have had special

The Lawe Top at South Shields has always been an attractive place for settlement. Archaeologists have found evidence of human activity from 7,000 years ago and the floor plan of an Iron-Age roundhouse from 2,300 years ago which would have been part of a farmstead. Excavation revealed a central hearth and a collection of hollows where the occupants probably slept, using heather and bracken for bedding.

It is believed an area near the door was used for food preparation to make the most of the light. A basket of cleaned grain and an iron woodworking tool were buried in a pit inside the house, perhaps as ritual offerings. The Roman army shared the judgment of past peoples that the hill was a good place to be and built their fort on the spot.

The fort commander lived in a Mediterranean-style villa 500 years later. Two-thirds has been rebuilt on the original foundations.

It had an entrance court, a courtyard with frescoes, a summer dining room, a dining room with underfloor heating for winter, his private quarters, kitchen, stables and baths.

It was the home of an aristocratic, career officer and is the most complete plan of a commanding officer's house in Britain.

One of the most arresting sights in the region is that of the reconstructed Roman bath house at Segedunum fort in Wallsend. Perched on the banks of the Tyne, it is the mirror image of the bath house which stood at Chesters fort in Northumberland.

But what makes the view so dramatic are the huge shipyard cranes behind the bath house.

Segedunum curator Geoff Woodward says: "I love the contrast. The cranes are monumental and they and the bath house represent two great civilisations."

The Romans chose the fort site partly for its views up and down the river. Fragments of inscriptions raise the possibility of a large monument to mark the end of Hadrian's Wall. The name Segedunum means "strong" or "victory" fort. The garrison in the Third and Fourth Centuries was the Fourth Cohort of Lingones, from eastern France, while a Second-Century garrison may have been the Second Cohort of Nervians, who originated from Belgium.

"It is one of the sites we know most about anywhere in the Roman Empire," says Geoff.

It sits next to the Swan Hunter shipyard and in the 19th Century was covered by terraced housing. In the 1970s, the terraces were demolished and new homes were planned.

A dig led by Charles Daniels of Newcastle University revealed how much of the fort remained and in a far-sighted decision North Tyneside Council opted to leave the site free of development.

Excavations uncovered the evolution of the fort over 300 years and in 2000 the £9m Segedunum fort, museum and bath house was opened, winning four awards in its first year.

Left: Segedunum Bath House with the modern back drop of the Tyne Shipyards.

Above: Segedunum viewing tower.

skills in river navigation and boatmanship which were probably used in safeguarding the mouth of the Tyne and the adjacent coastline."

South Shields has produced one of the largest collections of objects from any military site in Roman Britain.

The fort had been under farmland for more than 1,000 years. In 1875, the Ecclesiastical Commissioners made the land available for housing, which prompted a dig that uncovered Roman remains.

As the house building began, many more discoveries were made, such as the tombstone put up by Barates, a man from the desert city of Palmyra in Syria, to his wife and former slave Regina, who came from the Catuvellauni tribe in southern England. It shows what a cosmopolitan place South Shields must have been. Another tombstone was erected by a cavalryman to his slave Victor.

Clearance of the same housing sparked digs in the 1960s and in 1975 the fort was taken over by Tyne and Wear Museums and now attracts 100,000 visitors a year. Annual excavations have continued since 1977, aided in recent years by volunteers from around the world through the Earthwatch organisation.

The fort is the site of the longest-running research excavations in Britain, says Nick.

Even so, he reckons that at the current rate of digging there is a century of work remaining.

As well as the finds, another major draw is the reconstructions of the fort's eastern gateway, the commander's villa and a barrack block. "It is the only Roman fort site in Britain where you can see reconstructed buildings on the site of the originals inside the fort," says Nick.

Occupation of the Arbeia site continued after Roman rule ended in Britain.

Although the West Gate went out of use in the early Fifth Century, the partly-ruined entrance was later brought back into use, this time with a timber entry.

The fort was probably used as a stronghold to control the surrounding countryside and a pit was found containing the bones of two young men with weapon cuts to their skulls. The latest research suggests the site may have been the birthplace of Oswin, the Seventh-Century King of Deira, which later merged with Bernicia to form the kingdom of Northumbria. Finds from Arbeia have included a gilded bronze mount, perhaps from a book or a horse harness, a writing stylus, gaming pieces and dress pins. These have led archaeologists to speculate that the fort later became a royal site.

Near Segedunum a section of Hadrian's Wall has been recreated to show visitors how it would have looked 1,800 years ago. It stands next to an excavated 250ft-long stretch of the Wall itself, where digging is continuing. This has shown that there were several instances of collapse and repair.

But the extent of the remains, up to eight courses high, illustrates the potential for the preservation of the Wall in other parts of urban Tyneside.

The fort features a monument bearing 129 names of Romans known to have worked on the building of Hadrian's Wall. These come from stones erected by work groups and which name the centurion in charge of the gang. The fort had about 100 commanders over three centuries.

Arbeia fort in Baring Street, South Shields, is open Easter to September, Monday to Saturday, 10am-5.30pm, Sunday 1pm-5pm. October 1 to Easter, 10am-4pm, closed Sunday.

Entrance to the fort is free but there is a small charge for the Time Quest feature.

Tel: (0191) 456 1369.

Segedunum fort in Buddle Street, Wallsend, with shop and café, is open April 1 to August 31, Monday to Sunday 9.30am-5.30pm. September 1 to October 31 10am-5pm Monday to Sunday. November 1 to March 31, 10am-3.30pm Monday to Sunday.

Adults £3.50, £1.95 concessions, £9 family ticket. Tel: (0191) 236 9347.

Above and top right: Wallington Hall.
Right: An interior view of Wallington.

Wallington

Due to centuries of Border warfare, the building of grand country houses in Northumberland never reached the level it did in safer parts of England. But Wallington was one great house which bucked the trend.

The National Trust property, which has just benefited from a £1.7m facelift, is an ideal mix of history set in a 13,000-acre estate with walks and wildlife, a walled garden, ornamental ponds, the trust's first farm shop selling local produce, gift shop, restaurant and cafe.

Indeed, Wallington, including the picturesque village of Cambo, is the largest country estate protected by the trust.

House and collections manager Lloyd Langley describes Wallington as "the jewel in the crown of Northumberland."

The restoration has included returning to Victorian colour schemes, using the evidence of old paint scrapings, and the weaving of new carpets based on the 19th Century originals.

The house's spectacular china collection - one of the best held by the trust - has been redisplayed, with the core being formed by

Left: Wallington Clock Tower.

Above: One of the dramatic North-East scenes painted by William Bell Scott.

the array of porcelain brought as a dowry to Wallington by Maria Wilson, when she married owner John Trevelyan in 1791. Maria also inherited the museum, or Cabinet of Curiosities, built up by her mother Jane, who in one year travelled almost 2,000 miles by coach on fossil hunting trips.

The collection has been added to at Wallington over the years and includes everything from preserved exotic fish and tribal spears to part of the plank from HMS Victory on to which the wounded Nelson fell and part of the skull of a man who died in a poaching affray at Alston in Cumbria.

There is also a collection of 17 large dolls' houses, including the 7ft long Hammond House, which were used to teach girls about home economics.

In the grand Central Hall, designed by John Dobson, the North-East's celebrated 19th Century architect, are the dramatic paintings of episodes in North-East history by Tyneside artist William Bell Scott.

His works were commissioned by the Trevelyans and he judiciously included several of the family as historic characters in the paintings.

Wallington, then, is full of surprises.

Many country houses are hidden by walls, trees or long drives, but once visitors cross James Paine's delightful 18th Century bridge over the River Wansbeck, the house

almost immediately comes into full view, with its lawn fronted by grinning griffins' heads. These stone carvings were brought by ship to Tyneside from London by Sir Walter Blackett.

The Blacketts preceded the Trevelyans at Wallington. But before the Blacketts came the Fenwicks, who turned fighting the Scots into an art form. And the Fenwicks knew how to party. Sir John Fenwick's wild spending led him to sell Wallington to the wealthy Newcastle merchant and mine owner Sir William Blackett.

Sir John paid for his Jacobite beliefs by being

The outdoor charms of Wallington feature the walled garden, with its 1762 Owl House pavilion.

Its attractions include the Conservatory, built as a winter garden in 1908 and now full of the scent of heliotrope, and with banana and weeping figs providing a backdrop to a range of blooms. Outside, pale borders shade into hot colours.

The East and West woods were planted in the 1730s as

beheaded after being accused of plotting against William III. But he had his posthumous revenge. Sir John was said to be the first to produce a pure-bred British racehorse and part of the grounds at

a setting for the remodelled building. Now a walk leads to a new hide near ponds in the West Woods, where feeding stations enable visitors to watch a free wildlife display. Another walk leads from the house to the River Wansbeck. In the East Woods is the serene China Pond.

The farm shop is outside the gates to give full access by the public. The restaurant operation provides cakes and pastries.

Wallington was laid out to exercise his thoroughbreds. His top racehorse, White Sorel, was confiscated by William III but as he rode it at Hampton Court the horse stumbled on a molehill and the king was killed by the fall. This was the origin of the Jacobite toast "to the little gentleman in black velvet."

Much of Wallington today is the work of Sir Walter Calverley Blackett who by the mid-18th Century had largely remodelled the building and completed the Clock Tower, one of Wallington's finest features.

On his death, Wallington was left to his sister's son, John Trevelyan. Then under Sir Walter Calverley Trevelyan and his wife Pauline, Wallington became the centre of a Pre-Raphaelite group of writers and artists.

A later Trevelyan, Sir Charles, became a Labour MP for Newcastle Central and president of the Board of Education.

He opened parts of the house to the public in 1929, and gave Wallington to the National Trust in 1941.

He said: " As a socialist, I am not hampered by any sentiment of ownership. I am prompted to act by satisfaction at knowing that the place that I love will be held in perpetuity for the people of my country."

His words have rung true, for when the property was first opened to the public by Sir Charles Trevelyan in 1934 Wallington was visited by 700 people. Now the annual figure is 130,000.

The unusual Griffin Heads at Wallington.

The £1.7m to upgrade the house has come from National Trust central funds as the income from visitors fails to cover even the day to day care of a historic home like Wallington. During the course of the refurbishment:

5,000 individual items have been recorded, protected, packed and unpacked.

The roof has been repaired and all major services renewed. A lift has been installed to open up access to the first floor.

The massive weight of the elaborate 18th Century plasterwork ceiling in the library, which was in danger of collapse, has been supported by the use of 80 metal dowels to pin the ceiling to metal braces.

The Wallington gardens and estate are open all year, as is the farm shop. The house is open from April 1-September 5 from 1pm to 5.30pm, and from September 6-October 31 from 1pm -4.30pm. It is closed on Tuesdays.

The walled garden opens from 10am-7pm from April 1-September 30, and closes at 6pm during October and 4pm from November to March.

The shop and restaurant open at 10.30am-5.30pm from April 1-September 5, and from February 16-March 31. They close an hour earlier from September 6 – February 14. The farm shop is open seven days a week from 10.30pm, closing at 5pm from April 1 – December 24 and 4pm from December 28-March 31.

Wallington is 12 miles west of Morpeth on the B6343, or six miles north west of Belsay on the A696, taking the B6342 to Cambo.

Admission is £7, child £3.50, family £17.50. Garden and grounds only: £5, child £2.50, family £12.50. Telephone 01670 773 600. Info line 01670 773 967. Farm shop 01670 773 619. Restaurant 01670 774 420.

Chillingham Castle

House makeovers are one thing. Taking a thoroughly derelict, roofless and floorless medieval castle and restoring it is quite another. That was the challenge facing Sir Humphry Wakefield when he acquired Chillingham Castle in Northumberland from his brother-in- law in 1982. Sir Humphry is fond of likening the castle to an elephant.

"When I acquired Chillingham Castle I saw a pile of elephant bones. It has been quite expensive in time, energy and cash to put them all together," he says by way of understatement.

Because of that time, energy and cash, 25,000 visitors a year now enjoy the castle. It is, like its owner, rather eccentric - a description which Sir Humphry doesn't mind. Every nook, cranny and corner is packed with the most varied assortment of items the visitor is ever likely to see in one place.

There are objects under and on tables, on windowsills and hanging from and leaning against walls.

I started to make a list until, faced with a sea of miscellaneous bits and pieces, I gave up. I did get as far as a tiger skin, a fossilised bull's skull claimed to be 1.5 million years old from the Danube, a harp, model ship, Lewis

Left: James I room at Chillingham Castle.

machine guns, axes, swords and shields, Buddhist banner, a Saracen helmet, Eton suits, uniforms, birds egg collection, piles of magazines from the Boer and Second World wars, an aeroplane propellor....

My will to go on gave out when confronted with a combination of a handwritten records ledger for the Chinese Engineering and Mining Company from 1912 and a vintage sign from the Southern railway titled "They Steal Your Light" and expounding: "During recent weeks thousands of bulbs have been stolen from Southern Railway trains."

King Henry III stayed at Chillingham in what was probably a manor house in 1255.

There was a tower at Chillingham when Edward I stopped over on his way in 1298 to give battle to the Scots.

In 1344, royal leave was given to convert Chillingham into a castle. What was created was a heavily walled courtyard with a tower at each corner. They were needed.

Border unrest meant that in 1353 it was reported that only four of the 22 farms on the estate were tenable, the rest having been wasted.

The Grey family was in possession of the castle and in 1409 Ralph Grey captured the French castle of Tanquaville and was rewarded with the Earldom of Tankerville.

Chillingham Castle came under attack in 1536 from rebels opposed to Henry VIII when the walls were damaged by cannon fire.

King James I of England and VI of Scotland came visiting in 1617.

In 1823 Sir Jeffrey Wyatville, who had just finished working on Windsor Castle, arrived at Chillingham.

He was responsible for extensive alterations at Chillingham, including new avenues, lodges and park gates, and the Italian garden.

Two marble chimney pieces were brought from Wanstead House, which had been demolished in 1822.

The family stayed at Chillingham until 1932. The death duties and the cost of maintenance forced the Eighth Earl and Lady Tankerville to move into a house in the village. From then the castle began to deteriorate and the situation worsened when it was used by the military during the Second World War, when there are records of panelling being burned to keep winter fires going.

The unique tea room at Chillingham.

The mix is spiced with notes left for visitors by Sir Humphry himself. One describes how the fallen ceiling in the James I room had to be winched back into position.

Another reads: "When I came there were no floors or ceilings, just pigeon mess by the tonne."

It is a theme to which Sir Humphry returns in his handwritten introduction in the slim guide to the castle: "Forgive any disorder by thinking and knowing that I rescued a roofless, floorless wreck of a castle and jungle having taken over the garden and grounds."

Sir Humphry says of the notes: "I just want to say to each visitor do you like this or that, and take a look at this. I want to entice and lead people on." To the dungeon perhaps, where twisted straw figures are the victims of torture equipment.

But before moving on, mention must be made of the tea room. It is a tea room like no other. A tea room with attitude, with old castle stone walls hung with weapons and flags, unfeasibly large antlers, a great fireplace burning logs, faded tapestries. You can imagine 14th Century soldiery snatching a quick mess of potage in exactly similar surroundings.

Sir Humphry, baronet, international art dealer, businessman, adventurer, horseman is, however, back to elephants.

"When I saw the place I could see that the hip bones connected to the thigh bones. I just wanted to get my hands on the bones.

"It is not enough just to sit there and become a stockbroker or something, and retire gently. You have to do more.

"Chillingham is like sitting on the back of an elephant and what I have done is to feed the elephant for a generation."

Before coming to Chillingham, Sir Humphry had the benefit of a dry run when he lived in and helped to restore Lough Cutra Castle in Galway in Ireland.

Chillingham came into his life when he married Lady Katharine, the daughter of Lady Mary Grey. The powerful Grey family owned the castle for centuries.

He describes the surprises which have come through peeling back the layers of the castle and putting the pieces back together again.

"We have taken off plasterwork and found the slots for firing arrows.

"In the 19th Century people prettied up places

St Peter's Church, Chillingham.

but beneath that surface there is an ancient place and that is what I want to present."

In the Dining Room, it was found that a 16th Century chimney was covered by an 18th Century chimney and by a 19th Century version.

Near the Edward I room at the top of the castle, from which there are fine views of the formal Italian garden rescued from the "jungle", a chimney and fireplace had been walled in when a staircase was built. When it was broken open, around 150 documents dating from 1549-1656 concerning the Grey family were discovered, including letters from William Cecil, chief minister to Elizabeth I.

The recovery of Chillingham Castle adds another attraction to, and is an intrinsic part of, a Northumberland for which Sir Humphry has a very fond regard. He is anxious that it is not spoiled by over-development. "We should put barbed wire around Northumberland and charge people £100 to come in."

Finally, Sir Humphry sums up the philosophy which has led him to rescue two castles.

"Dare to fail is a lovely motto," he says. "Even if you do fail, you have experienced the journey, and you will have had some excitement."

Chillingham Castle is signposted from the A697 just south of Wooler and can also be reached on the B6346 from Alnwick.

It is open from May to the end of September.

The tea room and gardens are open from 12pm to 5pm and the castle from 1pm-5pm.

Admission £6 adults, £5.50 senior citizens, £3 children, £1 under-5s.

Telephone (01668) 215359.

The Chillingham Cattle

At the last count, there were just 73 of them in the world.

They have captivated greats from Victorian animal painter Sir Edwin Landseer and North-East engraver Thomas Bewick to one of the North East's leading wildlife artists, James Alder.

They were also objects of attention for Charles Darwin and have featured on national postage stamps.

They are the wild white cattle of Chillingham in Northumberland.

The herd has lived in isolation behind the walls of its 340-acre park for centuries - around 700 years according to the Chillingham Wild Cattle Association.

Many believe that they are descended from the auroch - the wild oxen which stood 6ft at the shoulder and were written about by Julius Caesar in his account of his Northern European campaigns.

Today, scientifically, they are something of a marvel.

DNA samples from the hair roots of individuals who have died have shown that the cattle are natural clones. They are genetically identical.

And this is not their only claim to special status.

"Of the 1.2 billion cattle in the world, they are almost certainly the only ones that live a natural life, and the only ones to have remained free of any human interference or management, and are the closest to their wild prehistoric ancestors in the way that they live," says Professor of Animal Science Stephen Hall.

"In this respect, Northumberland is uniquely favoured in the world."

It is believed that when royal approval was given in the 13th Century to turn whatever building was at Chillingham into a castle and for a park wall to be built, the cattle were sealed off for food and hunting.

Measures have been taken to give the Chillingham cattle the best possible chance of survival.

After the foot and mouth outbreak of the 1960s, a reserve herd was started in Scotland using Chillingham animals.

The cattle breed all year round and when productivity is good the reserve herd is added to, and now numbers 17.

But in recent years there have been scares.

In the last foot and mouth epidemic, the disease came to within five miles of the cattle and strict biosecurity precautions were enforced.

But in 2001, 15 of the cattle died when severe winter weather saw 3ft of snow overnight.

"Three cattle were killed by falling trees and the weak and the old died," says Austen Widdows, who has been the warden to the cattle for 14 years.

The herd fell to 34 but the birth of seven calves took it to 41 in 2002. The Chillingham herd now totals 56,

The Chillingham Wild Cattle Association has also bought almost 700 acres of the park and adjacent woodland after a public appeal for funds, which will help ensure the future of the herd.

The cattle had been in the care of the family of the Earls of Tankerville until 1971.

They were then bequeathed to the association, which had been set up in 1939.

When the 9th Earl died in 1980, the Chillingham estate was sold off but as a result of the intervention of the Duke of Northumberland, the park was bought by the Sir James Knott charitable trust and has been run by College Valley Estates, which is linked to the trust.

The association was granted a 999-year lease but has now purchased the land outright.

Due to the lack of interference, the area where the cattle roam is a largely medieval landscape.

"Fertilisers have never been used and there has been no ploughing. There are tangles of alder trees and we have been told by experts that their rootstock could be up to 1,500 years old," says Austen.

Long term aims are to replace conifers in the woodland with native tree species.

The association's cause is helped by a membership of more than 300.

Chairman Philip Deakin says: " The cattle are unique and that is why people think they are worth supporting.

"They are classed as wild animals and are remarkably free of illness. I think they go back to the original wild herds.

"The King Bull of the herd reigns for about four years and females are not sexually mature until three and a half so it is almost impossible for a cow to breed with her father. Nature has it all worked out."

Austen says: " They all have their own character."

He recalls an occasion two years ago when he saw an old female, who was 12 or 13, suckling a calf.

"She seemed to be too old to have a calf but she turned out to be a doting grandmother who had sympathetically come into milk and she suckled that calf for months."

Wildlife artist James Alder chose to feature the practice of the calf being introduced to the herd for his painting of the cattle.

James was invited by the wild cattle association to paint the herd.

He was following in the footsteps of Monarch of the Glen painter Sir Edwin Landseer, whose portrait of Chillingham cattle was painted for the Sixth Earl of Tankerville and is now in the Laing Art Gallery in Newcastle, and Thomas Bewick, whose engraving of a bull is one of his best known works.

A limited edition of 500 signed and stamped prints of James Alder's painting is on sale at £85 each to raise funds for the association.

James said of his visits to the Chillingham park: "You are sitting on a bit of land which the ancient Brits sat on and the place is throbbing with all sorts of life.

"The cattle have a sort of restrained, concentrated power about them and you feel you are looking at something primitive and there is beauty in that primitive look, and something you don't find in domestic cattle.

"The Chillingham cattle appear docile but you feel there is a power which can unleash itself.

"You are seeing natural selection at work and this is a place which should not be tampered with.

"It is a jewel and hopefully it will be there in perpetuity."

Indeed, sharing the park are more than 100 wild fallow deer.

The idea of hunting cattle seems odd. But prehistoric men did, and the auroch was extinct in Britain by 1,500BC.

It is thought that the Chillingham cattle were hunted for sport until the 18th Century.

Philip Deakin, chairman of the association, says: " This lot can run and they are fierce, with big sharp horns." Sport enough, then.

The last individual to kill one of the cattle was the Prince of Wales, later Edward VII, in the 19th Century.

According to Philip, the Bishops of Durham were said to have had white cattle at their Auckland park. "But Cromwell's men ate them."

Also during the Civil War, the Chillingham cattle narrowly escaped a similar fate.

In 1646 there are records of complaints in 1646 that Scots soldiers billeted in

the area were chasing the cattle.

But they have survived, and the theory of their link to the auroch is a tantalising one.

"The auroch was a very wild animal which lived all over Europe," says Prof Hall, an authority on the Chillingham cattle and a member of the council of the association.

In 1862 Charles Darwin wrote to the Sixth Earl of Tankerville, who owned the cattle, on behalf of a Professor Rutimeyer, who

had been sent a skull of a Chillingham cow.

"The Professor feels pretty sure it will prove to belong to the race described by Caesar in the forests of Germany," writes Darwin.

"I think that your Lordship will be pleased to hear that you and your ancestors have preserved alive this great ruminant."

The auroch vanished after the first farmers arrived with their domesticated cattle.

But there could have been matings between the auroch and the domestic beasts.

Prof Hall says that DNA tests reveal that the Chillingham cattle have been inbreeding for a very long time - evidence of being cut off from the outside world.

Here again, the Chillingham cattle have proved to be extraordinary.

"Conventional wisdom is that a totally inbred population will die out," says Prof Hall.

This is because of the concentration of harmful genes and a decline in the general performance of individuals, not least in fertility.

But over the last 250 years, the herd has averaged 45 in number and has remained viable.

Autopsies on dead animals have shown no serious cattle diseases and cases of difficulty in calving are very rare.

Prof Hall says: " Inbreeding may have purged the

harmful genes and the cattle have not lost out in terms of performance. They are an unusual case."

Because of their isolation and the fact that they live out their full lives - males up to 13 years and females to 17 - their behaviour is of great interest.

They are more vocal than domestic cattle, for instance.

"The bulls make a low, rumbling lowing sound but they also produce a high-pitched hooting which has been likened to an old railway engine," says Prof Hall.

With a freer life, it seems, comes more communication between individual animals.

"Domestic cattle don't have such a social life," says Prof Hall,

There is minimal human interference with the Chillingham herd.

"There is no castration and they have a natural sex ratio of bulls and cows," says Prof Hall.

"We bend domestic cattle to our own requirements, but with the Chillingham herd we can see their social life, and they are very social animals.

"They are far more expressive than you might think in how they communicate with each other."

A particular set piece is the introduction of a new calf

to the herd.

"The cow will give birth and feed the calf away from the herd," says Prof Hall.

"When the calf is strong enough it will follow its mother to the other herd members, who will be very interested in the new arrival, especially the cows.

"They will gather round to have a look and will sniff and lick the calf.

"The continuity of the cattle over hundreds of years at Chillingham means that it is a remarkable and unusual place."

The Chillingham cattle attract around 6,000 visitors a year.

People can see the cattle between 10am-noon and 2pm-5pm expect on Tuesdays and Sunday mornings, by calling at the warden's cottage for tickets.

The cattle park is signposted off the road through Chillingham village and there is an information pavilion next to the cottage.

Chillingham is reached off the A697 south of Wooler, or from the B6346 from Alnwick, or the A1 to Chatton and then Chillingham.

Visitors are directed along the three quarters of a mile approach to the park and are escorted near the cattle by the warden.

The park is open to visitors from March 25-October 31.

Admission is £4.50 adults, £3 concessions, £1.50 children and £10 for a family ticket.

People can become members of the association for £15 a year or £150 for life membership.

For both visiting and membership details Tel 01668 215 250.